Men
Behaving Boldly

Born in 1965 in Buckinghamshire, Paul Wallis is a church leader whose work involves him in teaching, in training and in ministry to students. He speaks at conferences and retreats across the country and has broadcast on Radio Two's *Pause for Thought*, and Radio Four's *Prayer for the Day*. He is the author of the popular paperback *Rough Ways in Prayer*.

Ordained in the Church of England, he has worked for a wide range of churches, from high Anglo-Catholic to Evangelical and Pentecostal. Most recently he has helped to pioneer the 'King's Church Portsmouth', and is now pioneering 'The Jesus Generation', a church community in Bristol.

He is a keen Gospel and Rhythm and Blues musician and an enthusiastic cook.

Also by Paul Wallis

Rough Ways in Prayer (1991)

Men Behaving Boldly

Getting to Grips with Spirituality

PAUL WALLIS

TRIANGLE

First published in Great Britain in 1998
Triangle Books
Holy Trinity Church
Marylebone Road
London NW1 4DU

British Library Cataloguing-in-Publication Data

A catalogue record for this book is available
from the British Library

ISBN 0–281–05125–9

Typeset by Pioneer Associates, Perthshire
Printed in Great Britain by
Caledonian International, Glasgow

Contents

Acknowledgements

My thanks go to two men without whose input this book would not have happened. To my Dad, Rodney, for his guidance and his word processor, and to pastor and friend, Will Napier, for his example and encouragement.

This book is dedicated to Ant.

Introduction

What is *Men Behaving Boldly* all about?

What is spirituality for men?

Why, in fact, do I get the feeling that spirituality is really for girls?

Why are our churches such lame, unmanly places?

Why aren't we producing heroic leaders like in the good old days?

Why are young men today so restless and demotivated?

What is masculine fulfilment?

The chapters that follow are going to explore possible answers to these questions by retelling an ancient inspirational story. The story is that of the great patriarch, Joseph. Instead of treating it as a dry piece of history or as a scripture-text to be interpreted, I shall approach it as a tale crafted to tell us something about maleness. Each episode will trigger a train of thought, and each chapter will tease out the storyteller's covert teaching about a young man's ascent to adulthood.

You might at first glance think that this is not the story's primary purpose. However, the lessons that the story holds about initiation to manhood may well have been the reason for the story's shaping and retelling throughout the centuries before it was written down, passed on in the voices of rabbis to young men, fathers to sons.

I am not saying, 'This is the plain teaching of the Bible on what being a man is all about.' Rather, I think this is what the story of Joseph can teach us today. This is what his story lights up in my own imagination. In Joseph's story, I find good answers to the questions that are bothering men today, at the turn of this particular millennium.

The storyteller who crafted the Joseph story as we know it has not suffered the ideological upheavals and gender-wars of the twentieth century. He is not presenting a 'new man', nor proposing a retreat to traditional stereotypes, for he has never heard of either of them. He is not part of a 'men's movement'. Nor is he part of a 'women's movement', come to that. He is not a sociologist, nor a politician. Instead, our storyteller brings to us something from completely outside our culture and so he can be free to present us with ideas and insights that are new to us or we have lost.

Men Behaving Boldly is not a book *about* spirituality, it is a book *of* spirituality. You will find in the following chapters ten user-friendly exercises which will give you practical help in engaging a spirituality better geared for the male of the species.

1 THE UNINITIATED

Episode 1: The beginning of the problem

Many, many years ago, Israel was a man with 12 sons. Israel, whose first name was Jacob, loved all his sons, but he loved his son Joseph more than the others. Joseph had been born to Jacob in his old age – and, because of this, Jacob doted on him. As a sign of fatherly favour, Jacob thought it would be a good idea to make a very expensive ornamented robe for Joseph to wear. So he did, and Joseph wore it all the time. Thus it became crystal clear to his poor brothers that their father loved Joseph more than he loved them. Consequently, they hated Joseph and could not speak a kind word to him.

Now, when he was 17, Joseph had begun tending the flocks with his older brothers. But the young men didn't get on with him at all, and Joseph made a habit of going home to his dad, and telling on his brothers' behaviour.

How did such an inept young man as Joseph ever become Chancellor of Egypt? I mean, at 17, this was a young man who, without even realizing it, could wind up his brothers so much that they wanted to murder him. They were willing to see their dear old dad break his heart just to be rid of the boy.

Yet, 13 years later, aged 30, this same man had gained such strength and quality of character that a great foreign power, Egypt – a country that knew him only as 'that foreign slave who tried to rape the Captain of the Guard's wife' – decided he was the best man to lead their nation through 14 critical years. What kind of journey had he made, what had changed him?

Step by step, we will take this journey, which brought Joseph from immaturity and inadequacy to fulfilment and satisfaction. However, the seeds of the whole story – the key to Joseph's early weakness and later greatness – lie in Episode 1, so let's look at it more closely.

'Now, when he was 17 . . .'

For us, the age of 17 represents perhaps one of the most critical years of our personal development – it is right in the middle of adolescence. For the modern Western reader, it is striking that the story begins at the point of Joseph's transition to adulthood. In fact, in the culture of the day, adulthood was considered to begin earlier than this. Indeed, that complicated, lengthy process we call 'adolescence' is a rather recent invention, largely local to Western culture. Then, at 17, Joseph should really have been an adult in an adult world. He should have been working for some time by then, labouring in the pastures with his older brothers.

This would have been the natural context within which Joseph would have learned to operate as an adult. Perhaps about the age of 13 he would have left working with the women to go out to work with the men, and learn to get on with adult men in an adult male world. Joseph ought to have been well into that process of initiation. But, we read, Joseph did not get on with his older brothers; the process was not working.

The relationships that should have been welcoming him to the adult world, and providing him with some healthy role models, had broken down.

The story places the blame on his father. After all, where is Jacob in all this? Genesis 37.2 reads 'This is the account of Jacob', and, from then on, with the beginning of Joseph's story, he is utterly in the background. However, we know enough from the first chapter to realize that Jacob's relationship with Joseph and his brothers was far from ideal. If Joseph's relationship with his brothers was cool – indeed, the storyteller says 'they hated him' – his relationship with his father was too cosy. His father spoiled him and cosseted him. It was not an adult-to-adult relationship, which by that age in that culture it should have been.

Jacob is unwise to allow Joseph to tell tales on his brothers, and not to deal with the matter. Surely by doing this the effect is that Joseph will grow up thinking he's better than his brothers. It cannot but be divisive. We can guess only too well what Joseph's older brothers feel about him being their father's favourite and confidant.

It is not surprising to hear that Joseph's brothers hated him. However, although we might anticipate all this, Jacob does not – far from it. In fact, just to make the point plain to all that he really does think that Joseph is better than his brothers, he has an extraordinary, grand robe made for Joseph that he has him wear in public. That Jacob did this tells us a great deal about his level of tact and social wisdom. He does not seem to understand how people tick. He fails to anticipate the bad result. For an old man, he must be just a little naive. Further, that Joseph was happy to wear the robe – even to work – tells us a great deal about him.

So, we begin with a bit of a mess. Significantly, the mess is in all of Joseph's man-to-man relationships.

These are the relationships that should be serving to introduce Joseph to the adult male world. He should be learning to work with his older brothers and have a healthy role model in his father, but none of these relationships is doing its proper job. At 17 years old, Joseph remains the uninitiated in the adult male community, and he is bound to get into trouble as a consequence.

The modern Western male finds himself in a similar state of affairs. He, too, is left uninitiated, wondering, 'What is it that comes after youth? What is it that's supposed to happen next? Is there life after my 20s?' What does a young man have to look forward to as he leaves youth and enters 'full-blown adulthood'? The modern Western man has a gap in his psyche. His initiation to adult manhood has gone missing.

The missing process

Initiation to adulthood is the stuff of tradition and ritual in Aboriginal Australia, tribal Africa or South America, for instance. However, in the West there is no formal initiation. Yet, there has been in the past – structures in society and processes have turned boys into men. As we shall see shortly, even these have broken down in modern Western society.

However, this failure to find a welcome to adulthood is not something the modern Western man will notice at 17. It will not be until we approach Joseph's age at the end of the story – 30 – that we will realize we have not made the transition he did. This lack will manifest perhaps in the late 20s as an anxiety that the best part of our life is drawing quietly to its close to be replaced by something far less exciting. It will make itself known as a fear of what comes next. What does come after the 20s? What is there exactly to look forward to?

4

Ask a 20-year-old this question and he will tell you that there is only dull routine – nappy-changing if you've been middle-aged enough to settle down or get married, and the gradual decline of the body. Even if it is said flippantly, there is a genuine feeling that nothing very exciting lies beyond the age of 30.

Then again, how could a 20-year-old know what the virtues and benefits of full-blown adulthood are? He hasn't been there. That is precisely why initiation to the adult world has to come from adults.

Wayne Rice writes out of 30 years' experience of ministering to young people in the Church:

> I have always been intrigued that in cultures of the past, youth had rites of passage which moved them from childhood to adulthood. Following these rites of passage, the youth would be embraced by the adult community and there would be a place for them in the adult world. This is no longer true for our kids. The challenge for the Church is how to make that happen for our kids. They need to be around adults. You don't learn how to be an adult from other kids. You only learn how to be an adult from other adults.[1]

Church kids have an advantage over kids generally in that respect. Our churches are intergenerational communities, so there is the potential for a network of relationships that can make this process work – or, at least, work better – for our young men than it has done in our culture at large.

As Wayne Rice writes, it is only adults who can welcome into the adult community, but that phrase tells all. 'Adult community'. What adult community? That is what has gone missing. It has been gone longer than we think.

The missing relationship

In the eighteenth century, the British government introduced new laws to speed the industrialization of the country. The Enclosures Act made it impossible for sons to continue the family tradition of subsistence farming. The new generation would have to move to the cities to find work – to the cities where the new factories were waiting for them.

This was not an entirely negative thing, but it meant massive social change. As for male initiation, previously, when boys reached 12 or 13 they would simply have moved from doing work with the women to doing work with the men – just as Joseph went to work with his brothers. Indeed, with a smallholding, a boy would habitually work alongside his father. There, in the context of men working together, a new relationship was formed. That was the natural context in which a father would give his *teaching* to his son. They didn't go on father–son bonding camps, relationship seminars or male bonding weekends, they just worked together and learned to get on.

Industrialization put paid to all that. With some exceptions, such as mill towns and mining towns, boys no longer worked alongside their fathers and uncles – society became much more fragmented. Thus, the natural way of moving the boy from the mother's world to the father's world was confiscated.

We need to understand, then, that the failure of today's generations to form nurturing relationships between father and son is not simply down to the failures of individual dads and individual sons. The problem has been caused by massive social factors beginning some two centuries ago.

Some dads have learned to compensate for these factors by playing with their sons as they grow into young men, taking them fishing, camping or climbing, or to football matches or some other sport. However, not all dads can or do take the initiative like this. The result is not only poorer relationships between fathers and sons, but a loss to boys of their chief male role models. If they don't see their dads or see them work, boys will struggle to admire them.

If sons only ever see their dads when they come home from work – in other words, off-duty, tired and not at their best, perhaps tetchy and indecisive, all their energy spent – what signals does that give them about their own place in their fathers' world and, indeed, about the nature of adult life itself? It doesn't look so good. Without that role model, where will boys find the ideal for their own adult life? It is something uniquely special and life-giving when a son can say, 'I want to be like my Dad when I get older', but it is often the shape of our society that robs young men of that kind of relationship.

What we have is a problem in the way our society orders itself – especially workwise – alongside the disintegration of the extended family. Generally, we no longer live close to aunts, uncles, grans and grandads. We tend to be more scattered. Consequently, when, as is often the case, there is no father-figure in the home, young men no longer have the opportunity to keep the company of older men. Boys' natural role models and the natural contexts in which they might learn from their elders are missing. As the Chief of Police in Detroit observed, 'It's not that these boys don't have a positive male role model in the home. It's that they don't know any at all!'

The missing input

Matters are worse than that, though. It's not just that we have a development shortfall. Our upbringing is actually unbalanced. That is because most young boys are, in effect, brought up by their mothers. Sometimes the father is wholly absent – there is none. Where there are two parents, often work will take fathers away from the daily lives of their families. Consequently, the norm is for the mothers' presence to dominate in children's upbringing. It will be the mothers' actions that clothe them, school them, care for them, discipline them and socialize them. That first part of our development is still reasonably intact.

During this part of boys' upbringing, they will take on the mothers' slant – a female slant – on the world, on life, on their fathers, even on manhood itself. It will be women who teach them how to behave. Come puberty, a hunger grows to get their father's side of the story, to spend time with him, to get a man's view on manhood.

There was, in our more recent history, that mythological moment when a father would sit his son down and give him a little talk about 'the birds and the bees'. That was the English idea of male initiation 40 years ago. I'm not sure how closely reality tallied with the mythology, but at the least there was an understanding that, come that awkward age, fathers would step in to disciple their boys, to make some input to complement and balance the teaching mothers had already given them.

It is important to understand that the female education boys receive will include a female understanding of men – no matter how inadvertently this has been passed on. Now, if it is a truism that men and women do not entirely understand one another, this is inevitably going to leave boys with an educational shortfall. Where does that leave young men needing to find out what a real man is? Their mothers cannot tell them – the input has to come from a man.

It's not necessarily that boys' views of manhood, or of their own fathers, have been utterly defamed by their mothers' teaching. It's just that the understanding is incomplete. It cannot be anything else. If their parents' relationships have contained a normal quantity of stress and disorder, the chances are boys have been told at least once or twice, 'I hope you don't turn out like your father.'

Now, boys generally may agree that in some ways they would like to be different to their poor old dad. However, how exactly *are* they supposed to be? Popular culture won't tell them because it is still doing a demolition job on the image of the adult male.

Popular culture

Very seldom are adult males in sit-coms and commercials set before us as models of manhood to be held up as ideals, to be copied. The sociologist Robert Bly writes:

> The father in contemporary TV ads never knows what medicine to take. And in situation comedies – *The Cosby Show* notwithstanding – men are devious, bumbling, or easy to outwit. It is the women who outwit them and teach them a lesson, or hold the whole town together. . . . Many Hollywood writers, rather than confront their own fathers in Kansas, take revenge on the remote father by making all adult men look like fools.[2]

If that seems overstated, take a look at your television over the next few days with that thought in mind, and consider what the TV is telling you an adult male is. Also, it's worth noting how many books and films have as their hero a man who is either young or is boyish, who has not really grown up. All the superheroes fit into this mould.

Again, consider how many books and films portray the younger man as the hero and the older men as the betrayers or the lame ones – *Dead Poets' Society*, *The Graduate*, *Lethal Weapon*, James Bond films, *Superman*. . . . It's not hard to list them.

In *The Mission*, it's the young Jeremy Irons against the papal delegation. In *A Few Good Men*, it's the young Tom Cruise versus the corrupt, older Jack Nicholson. In the 1980s' *Superman* films, we watched the young Christopher Reeve playing opposite the destructive, villainous, older Gene Hackman. In *The Firm*, the young, dashing Tom Cruise is the honest lawyer playing opposite the older, jaded and corrupted Gene Hackman. In *Crimson Tide*, the striking, young, honourable Denzel Washington plays opposite the older, war-mongering, crazed Gene Hackman. In *Extreme Measures*, the young, honourable Hugh Grant is battling against the unprincipled, murderous, older Gene Hackman. (Poor Gene Hackman!)

The *Lethal Weapon* series is a very interesting case in point. Throughout this series of boys' movies, the young Mel Gibson is forever trying to rescue the cautious and sensible, older, married Danny Glover from the dread dullness of his domesticity. Young Mel Gibson is the change agent. Poor older Danny Glover doesn't have anything to offer. He is just a foil for the verve and spirit of the young hero.

Such books and films seldom cast the older men – that is to say adult manhood – in a positive light. The heroism of the central youthful figure is seen in contrast to the wickedness of the baddies and the dullness of the rest. Generally speaking, the male heroes of film-lore are not the respected fathers of stable families.

The damaged image

It is not just in fiction that our icons of adult masculinity have suffered. History, too, offers such icons and we have to realize that every time history throws up a high-profile bad man, it reflects badly not just on humanity in general, but on masculinity in particular. Thus, it has become common to speak in reference to history using the term 'the patriarchy', understanding it to be an inherently bad structure. It is used not just to refer to exclusively male leadership structures, but has also become a new shorthand for men as a gender or as a distinct force in society.

Once history is divided that way into male and female, every high-profile bad man that history has thrown up is then seen to reflect badly on the credibility, not of the societies which they represent, but of the male of the species; of the male gender.

Every famous male leader who has proved himself evil – every Hitler, Mussolini, Stalin, Caligula – damages our image of masculinity. Every leader who has let us down – Edward Windsor, Chamberlain, Richard Nixon – damages our image of masculinity. The problem in today's society is that we can scarcely find a high-profile male leader to admire. 'Admire' is a strong word that does not come easy to the modern mind and somehow seems inappropriate in relation to the contemporary figures before us.

I am not saying that to cast aspersions on today's leaders. The situation is that our basic confidence in public figures is now so damaged that to compare the merits of Prince Charles and King George VI or Bill Clinton and John F. Kennedy is really a total irrelevance. Our leaders today could be head-and-shoulders above the calibre of leaders from past decades, but the fact is they will never be venerated in the way Kennedy was. Our society has changed. We simply do not revere our leaders like that any more. Instead, we sit them in front of people like Jeremy Paxman and watch them squirm, loving every minute of it. We expect our leaders – still usually men – to prove themselves either weak, ineffective, untrustworthy or positively wicked. This is the idea we have become comfortable with.

It may have been the whole of a society that colluded with the various kinds of badness that different male leaders may have shown through the ages, but we have to realize that with each instance it is the image of the male and the credibility of male leadership as a distinct, necessary and good kind of leadership that has suffered.

The women's movement achieved much in reappraising the role of women in society. Men are just beginning to reappraise themselves in a similar way. In the last 30 years, men have had to face a great tide of criticism as a gender, and have been left reeling. Some of this criticism has been perfectly justified. Some has not.

Some have tried to reconstruct the male of the species – cobbling together a 'new man'. Now, I am not entirely sure what the current 'new man' is supposed to be like, other than that he is less distinctly male than his forefathers. The traditional image of men has been successfully defamed in the minds of young men today, but has not yet been adequately replaced. In other words, men are left feeling that they really ought to be ashamed of being male. As a result of the constant repetition of anti-male prejudices and sentiments and the fashion for advertising that exploits images of women violating men, men are imbibing a level of sexism that would scandalize our enlightened society if it were the other way round. We are right to defend women against such denigration, but the gender-guilt of men is such that we are far more hesitant to speak out when the offence is the other way round.

Some try to retreat into a defiant restatement of 1950s macho, chauvinist man, as if we had learned nothing from our reappraisal as a gender. The time is surely overdue for us to go beyond the alternative reactions of paralysed guilt or militant defiance in the face of criticism. The common criticisms are that men are felt to be aggressive, bullish, brutish, non-collaborative, competitive, hard-headed, pig-headed, rude, sex-driven, misogynist, self-indulgent, untidy, insensitive animals. What then are our virtues? On that point, once again, we're far more hesitant. No one is quite sure any more.

The current growth of new laddism may occasion humour when it spawns such comedy as *The Fantasy Football League* or *Men Behaving Badly*, but what it reflects is a real despair in the male of the species that he has anything truly great in him. Laddism says, 'OK, I am a bloke. I accept that all blokes are louts. If that's so, then hang it, I might as well go for it.'

Contemporary blokes are spurred on in that approach by a growing assortment of 'lads' mags'. Middle-shelf magazines such as *FHM*, *Maxim* and *Loaded* all distil the laddist philosophy. In effect, they seem to have distilled the imagination of a shallow, hedonistic, rampant 19-year-old and are successfully marketing it to a readership stretching well into their 30s. Perhaps the older end of their audience read these magazines to reassure themselves that really they are still lads at heart. It makes them feel more alive and more masculine than what they imagine comes in the phase of life that follows – a phase they will therefore delay as long as possible.

It is not just adult males who have nothing to offer, according to our culture – it's the whole of the older generation! J. D. Salinger's seminal book, *The Catcher in the Rye*, published in 1951, put into the thoughts of its central character a feeling that was to become dominant in the 1960s and has stayed in our blood ever since – namely, that all adults are fakes, phoneys, compromised, untrustworthy and untrue to the high aspirations of youth. As we age, there looms the threat that we will become just like them.

Leaders of the hippie culture of the 1960s, such as Timothy Leary, introduced the adage 'Never trust anyone over 30'. It was meant in all seriousness. The people who first imbibed that doctrine are now old enough to be the 'untrustworthy' ones and young people today still feel the same mistrust.

In the same way that high-profile bad men damage our positive feelings towards manhood, so corporate icons of authority – such as the state, the government, the legal system – damage our aspirations towards responsible adulthood. If those institutions represent the adult world, perhaps we would rather be like Peter Pan or Superman and never grow up.

If it is older men that younger men need to teach them how to come to fulfilment as adults, we need first to allow into our own minds the belief that older men still have something to offer us. Only then can we seek to build teaching and nurturing relationships between the generations.

EXERCISE 1

1 Write a postcard-size paragraph describing your own father or whichever man has played the greatest part in your upbringing – be he a stepfather, uncle, brother, grandfather, pastor.
2 Make a short list of his strengths and virtues.
3 Make a short list of his weaknesses and faults.

4 List the things you believe he has given you emotionally and psychologically that have been good for you.

5 List some things he did not give to you.

(Understand that every point, positive and negative, that you have listed represents a positive value and aspiration within yourself.)

6 Write a list that turns each entry into:

- a positive statement of value
- a statement of intent
- a one-sentence prayer.

7 Use the statements of value and intent that you wrote for 6 as personal mission statements for you to speak each morning and use your one-sentence prayers as set prayers for your daily devotions. Here are some fictional examples to give you an idea of how to do this.

My Dad excelled in his work and has climbed to the top of his field. He abhorred mediocrity.

- I value excellence.
- I want to work in my field to the best of my ability.
- Lord God, help me to work to the very best of my ability.

My Dad never stood up to my mother when she was out of order.

- I value the capacity to set boundaries in relationships.
- I want to be decisive and open in setting sensible boundaries in my relationships.
- Lord, grant me the confidence and strength to set proper boundaries in my relationships.

Joseph's father is not an active part of the story as it is told. He is not at all part of Joseph's difficult ascent to fulfilment. Very often it is the same for us.

Exercise 1 seeks to put the father figure back into the picture for us in a positive and balanced way. Joseph would have done well to aspire to his father's fighting spirit – Jacob had plenty of that. However, Jacob's deceitfulness with his own father and brother, and his poor social skills in managing the workings of his own family, were well worth rejecting. Joseph's Dad was a mixed bag of things for Joseph to admire and things for Joseph to reject. Most father figures are like that. The key is to use both the good and bad of that relationship in a way that will motivate, not cripple. Anxiety says 'I never want to be bad in the way my father was' and does not enable you to do anything positive. Indeed, it is likely to make you fight shy of becoming a dad at all. However, training yourself to say, 'I want to be good in the ways my Dad was and turn around the ways he wasn't' is a declaration of hope and purpose.

It is worth making the mental effort, because it is far more healthy and life-giving to organize your imagination around a positive emotion of desire, than a negative emotion of anxiety. Anxiety cripples, desire motivates. The purpose of Exercise 1 is therefore to focus your imagination and emotions and your relationship with God on a life-giving goal.

EXERCISE 2

Identify some slightly older friends who are in a stage of life ahead of your own. Repeat the steps of Exercise 1 with them as the subject.

Sometimes our anxieties about our own future life come from observing what has happened to people who are going into things before us – into work, into marriage, into parenthood and so on. We might look at those older friends and think, 'I definitely don't want to end up like that.' Exercise 2 aims to turn these anxieties into positive expressions of desire around which your imagination can organize itself.

We have taken some time in this chapter to think about the roots of some of Joseph's early difficulties. In a sense, the whole unfolding of Joseph's story happens in answer to these primordial causes. In the next chapter we shall look at some of the good things his background gave him, and come to understand why his descent into slavery was almost inevitable.

2 THE PARADOX OF SELF-ESTEEM

Episode 2: The dreams and the first descent

One day, Joseph had a dream. It was a dream about himself. He thought it would be a good idea to tell his brothers about it. 'Listen to this,' he said. 'Last night, I dreamt that we were all out in the field binding sheaves of corn when, all of a sudden, my sheaf got up and stood upright. Then all your sheaves gathered round and started bowing down to mine. Isn't that fantastic?'

His brothers did not think it was fantastic. In fact, they were incredulous. 'So you're planning to reign over us are you?' they said. And they hated him all the more.

A little while later, the young Joseph had another dream. Undaunted by his first rebuttal, he thought it would be a good idea to tell his brothers. Perhaps they would take this dream seriously.

'Hey,' he said, 'listen to this, I've had an even better dream. Last night I dreamt that the sun, the moon and 11 stars – that's one star for every one of you – were all bowing down to me. Isn't that fantastic?'

His brothers did not think it was fantastic. Neither, to his great surprise, did his doting father. In fact, to the delight of the other brothers, his Dad gave him quite a ticking off. 'Are you expecting your mother, your brothers and me to bow down and worship you?' he said. However, Jacob did not dismiss the dream, but kept it in mind. The brothers hated Joseph yet more, and their jealousy of him grew.

There came a day when the brothers were working at some distance from home. Jacob thought it would be a good idea to send Joseph to supervise them, but as Joseph approached the fields where they were, the brothers decided to kill him.

'Here comes that dreamer,' they said. 'Let's get rid of mighty King Joseph once and for all. There's no one around. We can kill him and dispose of the body in one of these cisterns. We'll tell Dad some wild animal had him. Then we'll see what comes of his dreams!'

So when Joseph arrived, they tore off his robe – the very expensive, richly ornamented robe, which he wore all the time – and threw him into the cistern.

Now the cistern where Joseph found himself just happened to be empty. There was no water in it. So when some Ishmaelite merchants drove by *en route* for Egypt, the boys saw an opportunity for some easy money. They pulled Joseph out and sold him for 20 shekels. Then they went home to their Dad. They handed him Joseph's robe – which they had dowsed in goat's blood – and said, all innocent like, 'We found this, do you think it might be Joseph's?' When Jacob saw it, he went to pieces: 'It is my little boy's robe. Some animals must have killed him. Poor Joseph has surely been torn to pieces.'

Jacob tore his clothes and put on sackcloth. He mourned his son for a long time and, despite the efforts of his sons and daughters, he was inconsolable.

What reaction is the storyteller expecting of his readers here? This is not an easy question to answer. Reading this today we might look at Joseph's behaviour – going around in that special coat, provoking his brothers not once but twice by sharing his dreams with them, exciting them to such hatred that they resolve to murder him – and might simply conclude, 'What an idiot!'

However, that was probably not the reaction of the story's first readers. After all, the story's original audience already knew Joseph as a great hero and patriarch of their nation. When they read of these dreams, they saw a God-given portent happening in Joseph's youth that they knew was true and would ultimately be vindicated. Neither did they have our cultural inhibitions about boasting. So, whereas our immediate reaction to Joseph in these first two instalments might tend to be negative, to the Hebrews, Joseph was a hero. However, the story itself stands slightly apart from both those reactions, calling for a rather more subtle response to the young Joseph.

First of all, it is clear that the boy has unusually high self-esteem – symbolized by the coat. Second, he is hopeful about his own destiny – he seems to have no difficulty receiving and believing those promising dreams. Third, he is tactless – he fails to anticipate the strength of the reaction his words would provoke in his brothers.

Joseph's attitude and actions get him into trouble – they lead to him being sold to the merchants. The subtlety of the story, though, is that none of the traits is wholly bad. In this part of the story, Joseph combines hero and anti-hero. In other words, the writer is proposing something to shun and something to emulate. In this chapter, therefore, we shall explore the importance of self-esteem, and how a healthy level is crucial to positive and healthy dreaming, while too much can be disastrous.

The need for self-esteem

You will remember Joseph's spectacular coat from

Episode 1 – what an extraordinary symbol of uninhibited self-esteem. Jacob not only loved his son extravagantly, he wanted his son to know that he loved him like that, and gave him a permanent symbol of his blessing on him. It was colourful, expensive and glorious, and declared to the world, 'I am different. I am the favourite son of Israel, my father.' More astonishing than the gift itself is that Joseph was happy to wear it in public. In fact, he wore it all the time. The story tells us, he even wore it to work. The young Joseph is like a peacock, utterly delighted by his own magnificence. He is quite uninhibited about self-display, boasting or showing off. We have this attitude taught out of us, but Jacob magnifies it in his son in the form of the coat and Joseph parades it.

This grates a little on the modern reader, because it is so far removed from our own experience. Joseph's self-esteem was perhaps excessive, and the way the story unfolds it would seem that the storyteller is making the same point, but we tend to the opposite extreme. Certainly British parents tend to be rather less lavish in their displays of favour and affection than Jacob was, not being so public about it anyway. Neither is it rare to find children and adults suffering from a chronic deficit of approval or affirmation.

Working with hard, streetwise, urban kids in 1990s King's Cross, London, such a lack of self-esteem and approval soon became quite clear to me. I also noticed how the deputy head at our parish school had an unusual ability to teach and discipline these often difficult children. She worked hard to learn the names of all 200 children. In doing this she took a step towards making each one feel significant. She also took pains to express approval of any good thing she was aware that a child had done. I could see the impact that these affirmations had on the children. They would stand up straighter and their faces would light up. It was like food and drink to them. When it became necessary to rebuke a child for bad behaviour, she wouldn't shout or intimidate – she would simply say, 'I am very disappointed in you.'

This withholding of approval had an astonishing effect on them, and sobered them far more effectively than anything else could have done. The children were visibly crestfallen when she spoke to them in that way. It was like they were being deprived of air.

Sadly, we're often better at the withdrawal of approval than the expression of it in our family relationships. It is a fact commonly observed by visitors that we British seem far more comfortable with verbalizing effusive expressions of love and affirmation to our pets than we are to our children.

I believe that this is a real flaw in the British national character. It is the opposite of the kind of upbringing that formed the character of the young Joseph, uninhibited and hopeful about his future. This flaw in our culture makes for people who are embarrassed, shuffling and apologetic. It is so ingrained that I believe we scarcely notice it. The story of Joseph's upbringing should challenge us to question our culture.

It is difficult to discern the positives and negatives of our own culture until we see it in contrast with another. If we compare the British and American characters (accepting of course that these are generalizations), we can perhaps see the defining characteristics more easily. In the aspect of self-esteem, the difference between American and British cultures parallels the gap between us and Joseph, so let us make the comparison.

Peacock spirit

I find that when I speak to North American children,

they look me in the eye and speak quite eloquently and confidently. They might even initiate the conversation with me. Sometimes their social confidence seems startling.

Next to the self-confidence of the Americans, which we caricature as brashness, the British do look somewhat grey and apologetic. I find, for instance, that American public speakers are far less inhibited than us when it comes to talking about themselves and their achievements. They are much more like Joseph. They are willing to wear the robe to work, and say, 'Look at me!' The British are taught that even when they have been highly successful, it isn't really good manners to mention it. Even when we have done a good thing, there's something in British culture that says, 'It doesn't do to make too much of it.'

We are the opposite of the proud peacock. We wear greys and earth tones so as to blend in and hope that we will not be looked at.

Ruby Wax – an American resident in London – highlights this difference of spirit between the two national characters. Here she is speaking of the advent in Great Britain in the late 1970s of what we might call 'Americana'.

Suddenly there were burger places on every corner. And each one tried to be more [American] than the next. You'd go in and they'd shove a bald American Eagle in your cheesecake, and a complete firework-display in your hot fudge sundae! Then this tragic looking English person would roller-skate over to your table, trying to have the pert zippy glow of the American. . . . You know that look where the lips are hoiked backwards over the head, so you're looking at a smile of wall-to-wall teeth. But they were English. They couldn't pull it off. They'd just go, 'Sorry, sorry, the food's not very good here,' and fall over.[1]

Why can't we pull it off? Because in the British culture we simply don't have the same 'peacock spirit', if I can put it that way. Perhaps Americans could manage with less, but we British desperately need more of the kind of spirit Joseph had. We would benefit from a share of his uninhibited self-esteem. Joseph knew his Dad was proud of him. He was unashamed. He felt good about himself. Joseph didn't have this positive spirit knocked out of him until he was 17. Most British kids seem to have lost it by the time they're six. How does this happen?

Shame

If we are not good with words of affirmation within our families, we certainly don't have the same struggle in expressing shame to one another. 'What is wrong with you? . . . You are a wicked child! . . . I am ashamed of you . . . You are rotten to the core . . . You're sick in the head . . . You should be locked up . . . I don't want to see you . . . You belong in a home.'

These phrases do not merely communicate something about the child's behaviour at a particular moment, but teach them that there is something intrinsically wrong with them. This is the administration of 'wrong shame'. It takes only seconds to administer, but its effects can be very far-reaching. It is often this, without affirmation to balance things, that makes us unable to hold our heads high, speak confidently and hope for good things in our future.

It is not uncommon for children to grow up believing

there are two kinds of people – good people and bad people. If a child has an average upbringing, the chances are they will believe they are a bad person. If their behaviour has been averagely good and bad, the belief that they are a bad person will have been communicated to them time and time again. They will grow up feeling ashamed – not of their actions, but of being themselves.

Modern culture suggests that all shame is bad. Indeed, much popular counselling stands on this tenet. The teaching of the New Testament, though, is more subtle. In the world view of the New Testament, there is such a thing as 'proper shame'. 'Proper shame' is guilt experienced due to specific bad behaviour, and it is there for a good purpose.

Paul speaks of it in 2 Corinthians:

> Even if I caused you sorrow by my letter, I do not regret it. Though I did regret it – I understand that my letter hurt you, though only for a little while – but I am happy now, knowing that your sorrow led you to repent of what you had been doing. You became ashamed as God intended and so ultimately were not hurt by us. For Godly sorrow brings about repentance – a change of heart – which brings deliverance and does not leave regret. (2 Corinthians 7, 8–10)

Paul describes the nature of proper shame perfectly. It leads to a change of heart and sets the person free, leaving no regret. The very goal of proper shame is freedom from harmful behaviour. 'Wrong shame' is when a person becomes fundamentally ashamed of being who they are and feel that, no matter what they do, they will never be good enough. It brings despair and entraps people.

For Joseph, wrong shame would have left him believing that, really, he had deserved to be killed or sold into slavery. This would indeed have been wrong. He didn't deserve it. His brothers' response was inexcusable. Proper shame would have him acknowledging that he had been foolish not to have anticipated his brothers' annoyance at his dreams of infinite superiority. As the story unfolds, we see that this was indeed the lesson he learned.

So many of us carry at least a portion of wrong shame within us, but we only become aware of it when we meet people who, for some reason, don't have any. We find that they can do an American smile. They can receive a compliment. They can believe that you like them. They are able to believe that God is wanting to bless them and not humiliate them. They can believe that God wants to work through them and make their life fruitful. They have Joseph's capacity to dream and desire, and expect God to approve of these things. They are healthy people who have a capacity for God to bless them. A lack of self-esteem, a feeling that we are not worthy, leads to great difficulties in relating to God in such a positive kind of way.

We have embraced 'worm theology' – a cartoon version of the Augustinian view of man, that no matter how long we have been Christians, no matter how sanctified we become, we will always be as a worm, scarcely saved, and then only by God choosing, through gritted teeth, to forgive our intrinsic wickedness. We do not find it difficult to agree with such a view.

However, there is a great deal in the Scriptures teaching that a Christian has a fundamentally new and positive nature. The inward change wrought in us by accepting Christ is so radical that Scripture describes us as being 'born again' (1 Peter 1; John 3) or 're-created' (Galatians 6; 2 Corinthians 5).

In 2 Corinthians, Paul writes, 'If anyone is in Christ, he is a new creation. The old has gone. Behold the new has come.' I often used to wonder what this meant. After all, when I became a Christian, I didn't experience a personality transplant. I still got ill, I still sinned, I still had spots, I still had moods. Yet, something was completely different. Bit by bit I began noticing the symptoms of a profound change.

That, says Paul, is what God does to us when we receive the Spirit of Christ in conversion. We will find that something deep inside has completely changed. Our defining energy has been altered. Our spiritual DNA has been reprogrammed. What makes us *us* has changed. As Paul says, 'It is no longer I who live but Christ who lives in me.' (Galatians 2.20)

Using the Scriptures

We in the Christian Church have an advantage, because for the Christian, the Bible is a power-tool in the reconstruction of our self-image and overall world view. When we call it the 'Holy' Bible or the 'Holy' Scriptures, we are making a profound statement. The Hebrew word that translates as 'holy' has a primary meaning. It means 'completely different, quite foreign; totally other'. Part of the power of Holy Scripture is that it serves to bring to our minds truths from completely beyond our culture and beyond our own personal experience. A number of Biblical texts are given in this chapter to set in the imagination truths that, if believed, revise our self-understanding radically.

To those who choose to accept the love of Christ, the New Testament presents a different view of ourselves, far more positive than our parents, teachers, peers and culture are likely to have provided. For example:

That is what some of you were. But you were washed [a completed action]. You were sanctified [a completed action]. You were set right with God [a completed action] in the name of the Lord Jesus Christ and by the Spirit of our God. (1 Corinthians 6.11)

This change produces side effects in the life of the believer. These side effects include learning to think differently and learning to desire differently.

It is God who works in you to desire and act in the way which pleases him. (Philippians 2.13)

If you remain in me, and live out my teaching, ask whatever you wish and it will be given you. It will be to my Father's credit, that you bear much fruit. It shows that you are my disciples. (John 15.7)

So I tell you, ask and you will get. Seek and you will find. Knock and the door will be opened to you. For it is the one who asks that gets; the one who seeks that finds, and to the one who knocks that the door is opened! Which of you who are fathers would give your son a snake if he asked you for a fish? Or a scorpion if he asked you for an egg? Well then, if you who are bad know how to bless your children with good gifts, how much more will your Father in heaven give the Holy Spirit to those who ask him. (Luke 11.9–10)

If you who are evil, know how to give good gifts to your children, how much more will your Father in heaven give good gifts to those who ask him. (Matthew 7.11)

What astonishingly positive promises. Often, though, we struggle to take hold of the truth of them for ourselves. Sometimes we struggle because we have been taught that we are not worthy of such beneficence – 'I want doesn't get' and other such phrases. However, it is a basic and fundamental tenet of the Christian faith that God's beneficence depends on his character and love, not on our worthiness.

Sometimes we struggle because we have been taught that there is no Godly desire within us, we are wholly corrupt, that 'there is no health in us', as we say in the Book of Common Prayer. However, the Holy Bible shows us that God is wanting to relate positively to that living part of us that desires and yearns and aspires. God wants us to want good things for good reasons. He is actually wanting us to ask. Such teaching is unavoidable in the New Testament.

Precisely because Jacob had gone overboard in affirming his son, when God gave Joseph dreams that one day he would be great, Joseph had no difficulty recognizing that the dreams were for him and about him. Most of us would scarcely dare believe it. We might even dismiss them with an 'if only' shrug of the shoulders.

To reactivate our capacity for relating to our Heavenly Father more positively, we need to make a decision, as adults, to reject wrong shame and build a proper sense of self-esteem, rooted in our relationship with God.

EXERCISE 3

1 Identify negative, self-deprecating or self-limiting
   thoughts that go through your mind habitually
   when you are dejected or stressed.

2 Next to each one, write down the beliefs you
   have when you are feeling positive that contradict those habitual thoughts.
3 Get hold of a concordance, or a friendly theo-
   logian or pastor, and find passages in Scripture
   to contradict your habitual thoughts and write
   them up in a notebook or mark them in your
   Bible.
4 Make a list of texts that speak of what God has
   done to you/for you, what he has given you as
   a result of your decision to receive Christ. (See,
   for example, John 1.12, 13; 3.36; 5.24; 14.23;
   1 John 3.1; 5.1; 1 Corinthians 5.18; 6.11; 6.19,
   20; 8.3; 2 Corinthians 1.21, 22; 5.7; Romans
   1.7; 5.2, 5; Ephesians 1.13, 14; 2.10.)
5 As part of your daily devotional pattern, medi-
   tate aloud on these texts you have chosen.
   Preach them to yourself and motivate yourself
   with them.

Grounded in love

Of course, it is not an easy thing to change life-long
habits in the way you think about yourself. I recognize
that old habits of thought die hard. Choosing to believe
and trust something new is the work of faith and faith
can be hard work. If, for instance, 14 years of schooling
have consistently taught me that I'm thoroughly worth-
less, it will take some work on my part to change my
mind and learn to see myself differently. The alternative,
however, is to let 14 years of schooling ruin my life.

For people who have been abused by fathers or
mothers or others close to them, it can be very hard to
believe in the love of an invisible God. I believe that is

why churches – communities of Christians – are part of God's way, for it is their responsibility to make the love of the invisible God real.

John the Evangelist writes, 'No one has ever seen God, but if we love one another, then God's love lives in us, and becomes complete'. (1 John 4.12) Following the same train of thought, Paul prays that those who hear him might have the power to grasp the full extent of God's love for them. It is a beautiful prayer and so I have included it here:

> I pray that out of his glorious riches he may strengthen you with power through his Spirit in your innermost being, so that Christ might live in your heart as you believe. And I pray that you, being rooted and established in love, might have power together with all the saints, to grasp how wide and long and high and deep is the love of Christ; and to know this love which is beyond knowledge, that you may be filled to the measure of all the fullness of God. (Ephesians 3.14–19)

It is only by being rooted and grounded in love together that Paul expects the Christians in his churches to be able to grasp the full extent of God's love for them.

Joseph found it easy to grasp the promise of God in his two dreams because he was rooted and grounded in the love and affirmation he received from his father. He didn't find it hard to believe good things about himself. That was the positive effect of his father's lavish behaviour.

If we as individuals are to recover our self-esteem and, thereby, our own capacity to dream, if we are to learn again to receive God's affirmation and believe his promise, we need to root and ground one another in love.

31

If a young man is unable to believe that his heavenly Father is wanting to bless him because his earthly father never did, then it will be a work of faith for that man to learn to believe otherwise. Nevertheless, as a friend, you have the power to help him take hold of God's love, simply by giving him the affirmation and approval that you can. You won't plug the gap created by what is lacking between him and his earthly father – a father leaves a unique-shaped gap – but you are more than able to make a difference.

Many young men project their need of fatherly approval on their girlfriends or wives, and then feel let down when the love of their partner fails to 'scratch the itch'. They might then blame the emotional short-fall they feel inside themselves on the 'inadequacy' of their partner's love. However, a girlfriend can only give a girlfriend's love, a wife, a wife's love. They cannot give fatherly approval because it simply isn't theirs to give. If the young man fails to recognize the real source of his approval deficit, he will, unwittingly, put an impossible burden on his man-to-woman relationship. The same is true of any of his relationships. Failure to identify the sources of his emotional shortfall will bring an unhealthy measure of dependency into all his relation-ships, setting him up for repeated disappointments. We should be careful not to expect a kind of emotional satisfaction from people that is not theirs to give.

Peer approval deficits

It is not always emotional deficits from fathers that we need to compensate for in adult life in order to repair our self-esteem. Much of our understanding of ourselves is derived from our peers.

I used to work in a university chaplaincy. One year, a young man we'll call Patrick came to the college.

Patrick was extremely withdrawn when he arrived. He would never look a person in the face. He would stare at the ground and shuffle his feet and generally spoke no more than his name and a whispered 'yes' or 'no'. He attended the college Christian Union faithfully, but by the end of the first year no one had heard his normal voice – just his name and an occasional word spoken in a whisper. He was at times in a world of his own and would wander off as if quite dazed.

What had happened to him? At school, Patrick suffered three major setbacks to his ability to make social relationships. He spoke with a chronic lisp. He had bad acne and thick National Health spectacles. You really only need one impediment to make schooldays an utter misery – Patrick had three. His lisp was so pronounced that he could not open his mouth to speak without his peers falling about laughing and impersonating him, and his teachers seemed unequal to the task of dealing with the matter. Patrick simply resolved not to speak in public.

By the time he came to college, Patrick had not spoken in public for over four years. Not surprisingly, this had affected him deeply. However, by the end of his three years' degree course, Patrick was a transformed man. You would not notice a thing wrong with him. All that was required to change him was two or three of us spending some time with him – something we decided to do quite independently of each other.

I used to meet up with him for lunch. At first, our conversations were rather one-way, but, bit by bit, over the weeks and months, he began to talk, ever more confidently and happily. He no longer had a speech impediment – it emerged – and he changed his glasses. After three years, you couldn't wish to meet a more pleasant, well-adjusted young man.

He had looked almost beyond repair, but all he

needed to make up the deficit in his self-esteem was the approval and unjudging affirmation of a few friends who treated him like a normal person. Such is the difference that we can make to someone, just by being a friend.

It is extraordinary how much damage can be done during a conventional school career. I have a friend in the clergy – we'll call him Tim. Tim suffered the disadvantage of being what was termed 'weedy' during his school years. This was a problem when it came to sports. The PE teacher would line the boys up and then call out a number of boys as team captains, who, one by one, would pick which boys they wanted on their teams. Tim was invariably the last to be picked. Nobody wanted him on their team. He was an embarrassment.

He was an embarrassment to his whole year, once a week, for the five years of secondary school. If you have not had this experience, you might not immediately appreciate how crushing such ritual humiliations can be. Tim's response was to withdraw behind the façade of being a boffin, casting himself in the role of nutty academic. It was an escape that inhibited and hemmed him in for some years.

Again, it did not take as much as you might expect to begin to unlock Tim's full personality. A slightly older Christian friend took him under his wing and, week by week, encouraged him, building in him the confidence to branch out and flourish.

Sometimes all we need to repair damage to our self-esteem is a little help from a spiritual older brother or sister, a friend or a pastor.

EXERCISE 4

1 Identify three or four friends – peers or slightly
older than you – who you can trust and who
know you at least reasonably well. Ask them to
give you a short list of what they identify as
your strengths and virtues. Explain to these
people why you are doing this exercise and ask
them to do the exercise thoughtfully. You may
be quite surprised and humbled to recognize
strengths appearing on their lists that you have
wanted to have, but as yet have not recognized
as being within yourself.

2 It may be that your church or Christian Union
already has a pattern of one-to-one discipleship
or of prayer partnerships. Is there someone in
your church whose self-esteem you could help
build, by committing some time to them, via
church activities or a leisure pursuit, such as a
sport?

Masculine self-esteem

Every man is motivated in some way by the idea of
heroism. In secret, every man would like to be considered heroic in some way or another. This desire within
the masculine heart certainly plays a part in men's
relationships with women. A man will want his woman
to give him trust, admiration and approval. In short,
consciously or subconsciously, he wants to be a 'knight
in shining armour' to the woman he loves.

A man will quickly become unhappy, unfulfilled,
and unmotivated in his relationship, if his woman no

longer allows him to take that role. By seeking to reform or improve him, correct him or mother him, the woman, even with the best intentions, can unwittingly communicate that she no longer regards him as her white knight.

Some of the ways a partner might demotivate her man sound very trifling – being overcaring, pointedly compensating for his shortcomings, being overzealous in checking that he has not forgotten such and such, helping too often with instructions on how to drive the car. The fact that it is so easy to wound a man's self-esteem might lead us to mock it as being nothing more than foolish pride. What it really highlights, though, is that a man's self-esteem is both extremely fragile and extremely important to him. Hurt a man's self-esteem and you really have hurt him.

The story of Joseph shows us both the virtue and the weakness that high self-esteem can bring. The virtue is a positive spirit, strong in faith and hope. The weakness is naivety, tactlessness and pride. We see a mixed result in Joseph and the lesson his story teaches us is to covet the virtue and reject the weakness.

The first descent

Joseph starts out by parading his own self-esteem in the form of his robe, wearing it even to work. At the close of this episode it is torn from him and sent back to his father, soaked in blood. Reportedly dead, Joseph is sold by his brothers, becoming human currency for Ishmaelite merchants. This moment powerfully symbolizes Joseph's fall from favoured son to shameful slave. It was a cruel and excessive response by Joseph's brothers to his showy behaviour. Perhaps his bad reports of them had been justified after all.

It was excessive self-esteem that had bred in Joseph

a youthful naivety – a naive man always fails to anticipate negative possibilities. He expects everyone to be as
positive-spirited as himself and is surprised when people
don't like him or suspect him or respond negatively to
his enthusiasm. It is this inability to anticipate the bad
reaction that produces the tactlessness of youth and
leads here to the young Joseph's sudden descent to
slavery. Thus it is that Joseph's journey into adulthood
begins with a fall, a loss of naive self-esteem and security. Note that his initiation to adulthood is not an
ascent but a descent – a sudden, involuntary descent.

We do not count it against him that he begins with
his head in the clouds – he was right in his dreaming –
but now his feet need to start to touch the ground. His
slavery will be the means of grace to achieve this. It is
as if God, in preparing him for the fulfilment of his
dreams, is saying:

> Joseph, you know about your greatness. Indeed,
> your dreams were from me, but now you need to
> know about your nothingness as well. You know
> what it is to have the love of your father, but now
> you must learn how to get on with the rest of the
> world. Joseph, you have known what it is to be rich
> and to wear a fine robe. Before we can go further,
> you need to know what suffering is.

What might such a fall mean for us? The significance
of Joseph's first descent was that it woke him up to the
fact that, notwithstanding his dreams of eminence, he
did not yet have the wisdom he needed to be a great
leader. He was not tactful or good with people. Perhaps
for the first time, Joseph is confronted with his own
faults and limitations. A fall for us will be anything that
has the same effect in our own lives.

Joseph's descent to slavery puts him in a situation

where he is no longer special or significant. Before, his sense of being special was rooted entirely in who he was by birth. He was Israel's favourite son, simply by being born to Jacob in his old age. Now he has no status whatsoever – and no special robe. He is a nobody. Worse still, he is a foreigner. As a slave, his only chance is to make sure he is a good slave.

Likewise, a fall for us is anything that undermines our self-esteem, communicates to us that we are not special and confronts us with our own faults and limitations. Falling may sometimes take the form of individual crises – losing a job, a marriage breakdown, demotion at work or a failure to be promoted, a professional dead-end, a criminal conviction, an illness. Falling may also lie in continuous elements in our lives – parents who shame us, disapproving peers, a critical partner. Even aspects of our contemporary way of life can communicate to us that we're not special, such as living in one of a thousand identical houses, driving one of a million identical cars, performing a job identical to those of thousands of others. These things subtly reinforce the message that we are not special.

When these forces outweigh a man's stock of self-esteem, he will feel that he is a nothing, that he has nothing great in him, nothing special to offer the world.

Joseph's story tells us that he had to be brought down to that place before he could find his true greatness. His true greatness did not lie in being his father's favourite. Indeed, in Egypt, he discovered that, out in the big wide world, his father's favour wasn't going to get him very far. He couldn't use it as a reason for promotion in the house of his Egyptian master.

To become fit for what was destined for him, this naive young man had to be brought down to earth so that he might learn to build his character from a more solid starting point.

3 DREAD, DISAPPOINTMENT AND DESIRE

Episode 3: Slavery

Meanwhile, Joseph had been taken down to Egypt and was bought from the Ishmaelites by an Egyptian called Potiphar. Now, Potiphar just happened to be one of the Pharaoh's officials; he was the Captain of the Royal Guard. While Joseph worked as a slave, the Lord was with him, and because of this Joseph prospered. Potiphar could see that God was with Joseph, making him a good and reliable servant.

Thus, Joseph grew in Potiphar's esteem and, before long, he found himself entrusted with the whole of Potiphar's estate. With Joseph as Estate Manager, Potiphar didn't have to concern himself with anything because the Lord made Joseph more than able to do everything that was entrusted to him.

This is a true development of character. The Joseph of Episode 1 would have balked at being a slave. We can easily imagine him repeating his first mistake and getting everyone's back up with statements like 'I'm not going to be a slave for ever, you know. I've got dreams. I'm going to be great one day.'

Some people do this with their faith – thinking and speaking habitually of all the things they want to do for God in the future, things that may or may not happen.

The future is not reality. Any fool can be virtuous and fruitful in an imagined future, but real spirituality is worked out in the here and now.

In this third Episode, Joseph does not do this. Whether he retains the hope of his dreams or not we do not know. What the writer does tell us is that God was with him – not to rescue him from slavery, but so that he might be more than able to do all that was entrusted to him. In this Episode, Joseph's relationship with God has less to do with his future and everything to do with his present.

The spirituality we can see in Joseph at this stage in the story enables him to not only cope with an unhappy present, but even to prosper while doing so. In this way, the storyteller presents a clear challenge for the reader.

In fact, it is at this low point in his life that Joseph starts to show his true mettle. In slavery, Joseph begins to demonstrate that he is indeed trustworthy and good. We see the first hint that Joseph's application and good character will ultimately lead to his success, for Potiphar recognizes the character of the young man and rewards it. This will prove to be the first of three breakthroughs.

So, what does this mean for us reading the story? The storyteller challenges us to face our own facts, rediscover dreams and learn how to hope.

Engaging with the mundane

What was it that brought such a positive development in Joseph's character? What was it that changed him into a young man carrying the makings of his success within him? It was a crisis. Being threatened with death by his own brothers and then sold into slavery seems to have sobered him up. In slavery, if you don't apply yourself, you don't eat. This lesson was not optional for the young Joseph. His engagement with 'the real world' was actually forced on him, he did not do it voluntarily. Therein lies a lesson.

There is in all of us a tendency to escapism – an impulse not to live in our own world. We watch TV and films, we read books and magazines – all involve us in other worlds. Entertainment generally serves us as a 'distraction' from our own world. We all seem to carry within us a restless desire to be somewhere else.

TV commercials use this principle all the time, as they show products that are part of a world tantalizingly beyond our own. If we acquire the products we will be in some way overlapping with that marvellous other world. The advertiser's skill lies in knowing just how to tap into this restless longing within each one of us.

Where does this restlessness come from? Essentially, we are reluctant to engage head on with our own world for two reasons – dread and disappointment.

Dread and disappointment

There is within each of us a dread of the boring, the ordinary. We do not want to live in a world full of the mediocre, tedious, trivial, small-time, prosaic, normal, insignificant. Deep down we fear that is what our real life is, or will turn out to be. If those are our facts, perhaps we would rather not face them, thank you very much – distracting ourselves instead with any diversion we can find. Only from time to time will the thought creep into our minds, 'If this is all there is . . .'.

Such an anxiety can creep into any human heart. Fear of never succeeding, fear of living and dying and making not the slightest difference, fear of being forgotten, fear of not being wanted, fear of mortality. These are all aspects of the dread that lurks inside, but which we

41

rarely confront head on. Indeed, these fears are rarely conscious, remaining instead as undercurrents of feeling.

We seldom engage with these fears directly, but they still remain and retain the power to shape our actions. How many men, for instance, have an affair in mid-life because they haven't dealt with their own mortality? How many of us boast because we are secretly afraid of our own insignificance? These fears may be under the surface, but not that far down.

Alongside this dread is the disappointment that each of us holds. If every one of us begins with dreams and desires, then, barring those who succeed 100 per cent of the time in 100 per cent of their endeavours, we will all have to face disappointment at some stage. By the time a man enters his 30s, he will be growing gradually more and more aware that some of his youthful dreams, if not already achieved, are beginning to look less likely.

He was not a millionaire by 25. He did not play for his country as a teenager. His relationships didn't progress as he had hoped. If he has a family, it is perhaps not as he imagined. His career is behind schedule. His looks have proved less durable than he'd hoped. His income and job security are not as he had wanted. He has fewer real friends than he had expected. These are his disappointing 'real facts'. Each man's real facts are different. Every man will have his own desires and ambitions and, by the same token, his own areas of disappointment and frustration.

The tension of hope

Desire is a fundamental fact of life. Every healthy, functioning man has desires. Indeed, every living creature has desires – food, sex, relationships, control. These desires are part of our created nature. They are signs that we are, in fact, alive. Temptation may sometimes

42

misdirect these desires, but the drives themselves are healthy, good and common to every person. We need to note that a desire is a frustrated desire until it is fulfilled.

Because of this inescapable connection between desire and frustration, some religions have proposed that fulfilment lies in the extinction of desire. After all, zero desire must mean zero disappointment. We may feel instinctively that the answer to life's disappointments is simply not to hope for anything any more. That, though, is a recipe for despair. It is emotional suicide. From a Christian viewpoint, it is also spiritual suicide.

By contrast to the spiritualities of passivity and the extinction of desire, Christianity proposes that frustrated desire is a proper part of our spiritual life. Indeed, it is a driving force. Jesus himself spoke of the steely determination of a widow who kept on and on at an unjust judge, until her persistence won her the justice she sought. Jesus gave this parable as a very model of the Christian's life of prayer (Luke 18). Luke says that Jesus told it to his disciples, 'to show them that they should always pray and not give up'.

Similarly, Paul shares his own yearning in his letter to the Christians at Philippi:

I want to know Christ and the power of his resurrection. . . . Brothers, I do not consider that I have yet taken hold of it. This one thing I do, forgetting what lies behind, and straining forward to what lies ahead, I press on toward that goal, to take hold of the prize for which God has called me heavenwards through Christ Jesus. (Philippians 3.10–12)

From this we can see that even the great Apostle was not afraid to confess his 'facts' – 'I have [not] yet taken hold of it' – or to admit his unfulfilled desire – 'I want to know Christ and the power of his resurrection'. Such a 'straining forward' is actually essential to a man's spirituality.

To bring him beyond himself into a place of fulfilment, a man's spirituality must engage both his real facts (his actual life) and his unfulfilled desires (his life force). Otherwise, he will not be tapping into what makes him truly alive.

Facing facts

Deep down, we are perhaps nervous of looking at our lives square on for fear of the disappointments we will have to deal with. If we choose not to face our own lives as they are, however – a mixture of happiness and sadness, fulfilment and frustration, desire and disappointment – Joseph's story warns us that we may find ourselves faced with a crisis that will force us to do so. Joseph was welcomed to the real world by a crisis, and this is often how it is for us, too.

A crisis arrests us. It may be an accident. It may be a death. It may be a move to a new job or a new town. It may be the break-up of a long-standing relationship. It may be an illness. It may be losing a job. Whatever it is, it stops us in our tracks and we find ourselves thinking, 'Is this really what my life is?' It comes to every man at some point or other, in some way or other.

How can we engage with both our facts and our dreams and desires in a more tranquil way, without a crisis to set the ball rolling?

EXERCISE 5

1 Make a list of as many elements of your life as you can – physical health, mental health,

---

relationships, family, work, career, location, housing, leisure pursuits, spiritual life, social life, wealth, education, accomplishments, creativity, sports and so on.

2 Divide them into two categories headed:

- 'These things in my life are OK'
- 'These things are not as I want them to be.'

(The first category is cause for thanks. Remember, too, that although each item listed in the second category may represent pain and frustration, it also represents a positive desire, and desire is a sign of life.)

3 Write a positive sentence for each item, expressing the first category as thanksgiving and the second as positive desires.

4 Use the exercise as a prayer. Read the words aloud to God, slowly and soberly, thinking the meaning of each word as you speak it.

You have now just completed an exercise in hope. It doesn't mend anything or make anything happen. It is simply an effective and practical way of making a decision to hope – especially if you do this regularly. You may not feel any better for having done it – hope is not necessarily any more comfortable than apathy. Indeed, hope is a decision for discomfort and frustration. However, in the sense that it reawakens both desire and self-control, it is a decision for life, a decision to channel what makes you truly alive.

What, after all, is the alternative to deliberate hope? A man could instead decide to 'come to terms' with his life. He could teach himself to hold only such expectations as have no possibility of leading to disappointment.

He might teach himself to expect nothing and so not be surprised when nothing happens. Where is the thrill in that? A decision not to hope is really only cowardice, and heralds death to a man's spirit.

We shall see in the next chapter that it is actually part of a man's nature to be aggressive, but to channel it. We have all around us the evidence of such an impulse within the male of the species. The problem is not that such energy is there, but that so often it is channelled destructively. It need not be, however.

It is as if every man has inside him a restless warrior, looking for a fight. The man needs to engage that warrior if he is to feel truly alive. Learning to do this healthily is part of a boy's growing into being a man. Such is the decision to hope. It channels the man's warrior energy.

If, instead, the man decides to make peace with his circumstances, never to rail at frustration, never to hope against hope or to desire until satisfied, he is choosing to suppress part of his masculine make-up. As a man, he is choosing unfulfilment. For a man, the decision to hope is a decision to come alive again.

Reappraising dreams

Facing the facts of our own circumstances is only half the equation, however. On its own, all it does is bring us down to earth. It could even be dispiriting in the longer run. Joseph could have let his descent to slavery bring him down to earth and knock all the hope and positive attitude out of him. He could have turned into a disenchanted, disappointed young man, who believed that the grand dreams of his youth simply had no place in the bitter 'real world'. Instead, Joseph learned to use his dreams differently.

When we reach the kinds of crises in life that force

us to face our own disappointments and disillusion, we, too, face such a choice. The first option is to come to terms with current circumstances and reject our youthful dreams and aspirations. We might feel embarrassed that we were ever naive enough to have been a dreamer and entertained such hopes. The second option is to reappraise the dreams of our youth.

Some of our youthful dreams will prove to have been no more than boyish fantasy – first million by 25 . . . married to someone famous . . . owning a beautiful yacht . . . driving a Porsche. . . .

Some dreams may have been more worthy – to be adored by my partner . . . to be my own boss . . . to be excellent in my field of expertise . . . to be known as an authority on some matter. . . .

Some might straddle the two – to be a company director . . . to be a famous author . . . to be indispensable to my community. . . .

Simply to reject our dreams is a clumsy and immature reaction. To sift and reappraise them is the better, adult response.

Just suppose the ambitions listed above were mine and that, at 25, I had achieved none of them. It would not be at all difficult for me to sift the fantasy from the good, and to decide what I should still be going for.

Of the first set, I might decide to retain the idea of the yacht. Perhaps I have actually never taken steps towards making the dream happen – other than vaguely hoping for a higher (fantasy) income, at which point I could buy a perfect (fantasy) yacht. Perhaps I need to take different steps – like getting to know some yachting people.

Of the second set, I may wish to retain all of them. These would be what I still want in my heart of hearts. I should not reject them as being out of reach if they are actually not out of reach. However, I must also educate myself out of the fantasy way of thinking – 'One day, these things will be mine. One day they will happen.' Clearly I have to make them happen, and I have to start where I am.

A happy and functional marriage relationship is, on full reflection, a good ambition to have. Therefore, rather than looking at my real, imperfect relationship and saying, 'This is not what I wanted', I have to learn to say, 'This is not yet how I want it to be'.

To be excellent in my field is, on reflection, a perfectly good and reasonable thing to go for. So, instead of considering my standing and saying, 'But I am not an authority on anything', I must instead make a decision, if it is achievable, to gain as much experience and knowledge as I can. I must invest in relationships with people in that field in order to build up the level of expertise I want.

I may look at the third set and conclude that those things cannot happen – unless I apply myself to the second set.

This, then, becomes my decided, adult response to my youthful dreams.

Some of my dreams may actually need to be reinterpreted before I can evaluate them properly. In my youth, I may have been motivated by the idea of being a famous leader in my field. It may have been pure fantasy. Lots of people want to be famous, after all. However, I may reflect that what I really wanted was influence, to be able to make a difference. It may be that, as an adult, I reject the ambition for fame, but decide instead to foster the kind of character and relationships that will enable me to make a difference, somewhere, to some group.

For example, in his youth, David wanted to be a bishop. Part of that ambition was the desire to have standing and position, but part of it was also a desire to be a pastor to pastors. At 38, David realized that, based on his rate of progress so far, episcopacy was probably not going to come his way after all. Now, at that point, he could have allowed himself to forget his dream and reconcile himself to his current limitations. Instead, he reflected that, as an adult, it was not the fame and the pomp of being a bishop that motivated him. Rather, it was the desire to make a difference to local church ministers; to pastor and encourage them.

The office of bishop may have proven itself to be out of his reach, but the substance of his dream was not. He simply needed to realize, on reflection, that he should be seeking to bless and encourage the pastors he already knew and who already valued his input. There lay his circle of influence. That was where he should apply himself, if the substance of his dream was to find fulfilment.

David's story is just a simple example of how a man can allow his youthful dream still to motivate him but in a different way. He is looking less at the superficial agenda he created in his youth and more at what kind of adult character he wants to become. Then he can make his reasoned response, starting from reality where he is now within his current sphere of influence.

Starting from here

Joseph's response to the contrast between his own facts and hopes was to make himself a good slave. He excelled in his given spheres of influence within the household. He did not look at his slavery and opt out, saying, 'I want a different sphere of influence. My dreams tell me I should be a leader.' Such a response would only have earned him the whip. Instead, he sought to excel in what influence he had been given. In the story 'the Lord was with him' and made him 'more than able to do all that was entrusted to him'. Because of this, Joseph 'found himself entrusted with the whole of Potiphar's estate'.

In other words, Joseph learned that if you apply yourself to your given circle of influence, it expands. The story of Joseph assures us that this is not only the truth of how people tick, but also represents how God responds towards us. Jesus himself taught that the one who is faithful in small matters will be trusted by God in great matters. One man who illustrates this approach perfectly is Jack Coe – a Pentecostal evangelist of the 1940s and 1950s.

In his youth, Jack Coe was devout and zealous in his faith, but, like the young Joseph, he was tactless and bad with people, to such an extent that the only way the Army coped with him was to confine him to the camp's 'psych' ward. He just seemed out of control. Coe believed that God was calling him to be a great preacher. Again, just like the young Joseph, his dreams were, ultimately, to prove right. However, first he had a few lessons to learn. Coe was not yet able to be entrusted with such influence.

Eventually, the time came when Coe had calmed down sufficiently to be posted to a camp that did not feel the need to incarcerate him. One day, Coe took himself down to the local Holiness Movement church, and announced to the minister there that he believed God wanted him to preach at the church.

The minister thanked young Jack Coe and suggested that he might like to begin by helping pray for people at the Communion rail at the end of the services. Jack Coe's pride was so offended by this humble suggestion that he left in a huff. However, at length, he returned and apologized, offering himself a little more meekly to 'whatever' the minister wanted.

'That's great,' said the minister. 'Our janitor has just

left. You can do his work.' Once again, Coe was sorely offended and stormed out. Again, God worked in his conscience and he returned the next day to agree to work as the church's janitor.

The minister was a tough taskmaster, but, having watched Coe learn to apply himself to the job he was given, he allowed the young preacher to take classes in the junior Sunday school (the children were aged nought to three). Coe was not elated, but applied himself to the task at hand. Having proved himself there, he was later allowed to serve as a worship leader, then later still as the youth minister. Ultimately, after an apprenticeship of some years, Jack Coe was finally entrusted with the entire church.

How shrewd Coe's minister had been. Coe's dreams were correct – he was indeed to become a great preacher – but first he needed the stuffing knocking out of him and some character putting in. Like Joseph, Coe learned that if you apply yourself in your given sphere of influence, God will have cause to entrust you with more.

Remembering dreams

As we saw in Chapter 2, most of us have our boyish ambitions trodden on at a very early age. We may lose our self-esteem and positive spirit very young. By the time we leave education and enter the world of employment, the fear of adulthood and the shuddering reality of the state of the jobs market are doing their work to dismantle our hopes of doing well. All in all, young men are leaving college and, far from being ambitious, thrusting, dynamic young hopefuls, they have already dispensed with ambition in order to avoid future disappointment.

Thus, by the time they begin their careers in their

51

early 20s, many young men feel that they have already come to terms with the grim reality of their actual prospects. There is no hope to change the world. This desire was, for generations, understood to be part of the spirit of youth. But our youth seem to have had it knocked out of them.

Joseph's positive view of life was not touched until he was 17. If we are to act as Joseph did and let our dreams motivate us in a new, more considered way, we must first do some work to recall what our dreams actually are because, for us, they may be long forgotten. So, how do we tap into them?

I once went on a prayer retreat to answer that very question for myself. The purpose of my retreat was to try to focus on what my passions were, so that I could organize my time better around my real priorities as a minister. My question was simply 'What are my passions?', but I was not sure how to find an answer to it. I could tell you what my enthusiasms were, but passions are deeper than that.

I sat in my cell at the Greek Orthodox monastery and found myself looking at the icons on the wall. It struck me that none of them moved me particularly. I didn't resonate with any of the people portrayed, but, thinking about it, I found I could name four pictures at home that did do something for me. They portray four people I really admire – St Paul the Apostle, St Seraphim of Sarov, St John of the Cross and Charles Simeon.

So, I thought about those four men and listed their traits. I realized that what this list represented was, in fact, my own aspirations and ambitions. I resonated with the thought of these people because I want to be like them – not only in character, but in the sorts of things I want to achieve before I die.

EXERCISE 6

1 Look for pictures, portraits, icons or objects in your home or office that reflect your dreams – past or present. Make a list of the hopes and ideas they each represent.

2 First, make a list of people you consider heroic or who have been role models to you in some way. They could be dead or alive; people you know or know about.

   Second, list the attributes you admire in them.

3 If you like reading, your collection of books might tell you something similar. They might represent passions that you have not acted on in some time. List the ideas that the books represent for you.

Understanding our values

Our deepest desires are not just a matter of specific ambitions and passions. They stem from our basic values. Exercise 7 will help you become more conscious of what it is you want at that level.

EXERCISE 7

1 Imagine that you are at a funeral chapel. As you look around the building, you can see friends and family, colleagues and associates. Little by little you realize that you are their common connection and that the body in the box is

yours. You are, in fact, watching your own funeral. Think about who is there.

In place of a sermon, four short eulogies are to be given – one from a member of your family, one from a friend, one from a colleague, and one from a person representing your local community who knew you less well.

What would you like each of them to say? What characteristics would you like them to have seen in you? What differences would you like to have made in their lives?

2 Write down two or three sentences for each eulogy.

3 Turn each sentence into a statement of purpose or intent. This gives you the basis of a personal mission statement that you could use as a focusing exercise at the beginning of each day. You could combine it with the mission statement you write in the first two exercises, modifying it, shortening it and including themes and rhythm to help you memorize it.

4 Speak it aloud before God as a proactive way of praying.

The result of this exercise is the exposing of your personal values. If you have said, for instance, that you want people to remember you as a person of integrity, you are saying that you value integrity enormously, that it is a quality you aspire to having.

I once asked a friend of mine, 'Stephen, what would you like people to remember you for when you die?' My friend did not suggest an achievement or an accomplishment. He said, 'I would like people to remember me as being kind.'

Later, on reflection, I thought, 'But if Stephen is being kind on purpose, does that count? Does deliberate kindness qualify as real kindness?'

As I thought about our exchange, I came to understand that, in fact, Stephen was not leaving his future to chance. Being a kind person was not for him a vague hope about his distant future – anyone can be virtuous in the future. For him, kindness was what he was choosing to do, in the present. He decided he was going to be kind now, by choice.

Keeping our deepest values at the forefront of our minds in this way can bring a depth, clarity and deliberateness to our decision making during the course of a day. It certainly makes it easier to make sure that our present actions align with our deepest values. In this way we can become people who are less defined by circumstances, more defined by conscious choice.

In those first years in slavery, Joseph made his response to the gap between his dreams and his degrading circumstances. He chose a response that helped him become a man worthy of the dreams he had been given. Indeed, to be a man worthy of his dreams might very well have been Joseph's own informal mission statement. Of course, he didn't have the benefit of this modern label for it. Perhaps he would just have known it as his hope.

4 VIRTUES AND STRENGTHS

Episode 4: The second descent

Now Joseph was very good-looking, and it didn't take long before Potiphar's wife noticed him. She took a shine to him and tried to get him to sleep with her, but Joseph refused. Though Potiphar's wife tried it on every day, Joseph refused to sleep with her, and took care not to be alone with her. However, it happened one day that Joseph was working in the house and none of the household staff was in. The woman caught hold of Joseph by his cloak and said, 'Come to bed with me!'

Joseph left his cloak in her hand and ran from the house. When she saw this, she screamed for help and her household servants ran in. She told them, 'That Hebrew slave tried to rape me, but I screamed for help. When he heard me scream, he left his cloak behind and ran out of the house.' She kept his cloak as 'evidence' to show to Potiphar. When she repeated the story to her husband, Potiphar burned with rage. He took Joseph and, without listening to his side of the story, threw him into prison.

Now, the prison where Joseph was held just happened to be the Royal Gaol. While Joseph was there, the Lord was with him and, because of this, Joseph prospered. He grew in the esteem of the Warder and soon found himself entrusted with the charge of all those held in the prison. With Joseph as Prison Manager, the

Warder didn't have to concern himself with anything, because the Lord made Joseph more than able to do everything that was entrusted to him.

Joseph now faces a second descent. The first descent was, if undeserved, at least logical given the circumstances. There was a cause and an effect. He upset his brothers, they reacted. Joseph could understand that. Then followed the first breakthrough – his promotion to Estate Manager and Chief of Staff. He had worked well, and he was rewarded. Again, this makes sense. There was cause and effect.

However, his second descent – wrongful imprisonment on a false charge of rape – was totally undeserved. Joseph now has to learn that sometimes life is not just, that it does not always make sense. Bad things happen to good people and vice versa. Suffering in a world that is so random is somehow much harder to deal with than when there is some logical reason for it.

During a short bout of unemployment, the DSS sent me on an 'Executives' Job-Search Seminar'. I can remember the sense of indignation expressed by a number of middle-aged business executives who were there. They were quite bewildered to find themselves in mid-life facing long-term unemployment. This was beyond their reasoning. They had done everything right. Education, training, experience, moving jobs but not too often. Yes, they had done everything right, but would quite possibly never work again. This was their welcome to the real world, and to the dreadful realization that life does not always reward us as it ought to. Joseph now had to deal with the same kind of bewilderment.

This second descent was a further challenge to the young man's self-esteem. Note that Joseph has lost a second cloak. The first cloak was returned blood-stained to a father who loved him and wanted to bless him. The second was taken from him by a woman who despised him, but wanted to use him.

The loss of the first cloak represented a loss of self-esteem. It signalled a rude awakening to his own faults and limitations. The loss of this second cloak signals the loss of his reputation. All men want to be admired in some way or another. They crave admiration, whether it comes as a result of virtue, cheek, charm or perversity – even sneaking admiration will do. We saw earlier that a man's basic emotional needs are for trust, admiration and approval.

On all those fronts, Joseph had been doing well. In his exalted position in Potiphar's household, he enjoyed all those things. He had been a good slave, winning the trust and approval of his master. With the loss of his second cloak, however, he loses it all in an instant. Now those who meet him will meet not just a foreign slave, but 'that slave who attempted to rape his master's wife'. Even the opinion of Potiphar, who had liked and trusted the young man, was converted, in an instant, to fury and rage. Such a withdrawal of approval at such a time of crisis delivers a very bitter blow.

Yet, even at this turn of events, we see that Joseph retains his good character and lets it shine through. Consequently, the Warder recognizes Joseph's qualities and rewards him with as much status and trust as the situation affords. Thus we know, and so does Joseph, that while circumstances have taken a bad turn, in himself he is still OK. The potential therefore remains for a happier future.

What reaction is expected from us during this part of the story? We hear first that Joseph has been working well in his master's house, that he has applied himself with character and diligence. He has demonstrated a wisdom and steadiness of spirit that are admirable. What, though, has been his reward? A second descent, this time totally undeserved.

Our first reaction might be to feel indignant on our hero's behalf, but what does Joseph himself do?

By the way, it's worth observing that at this point in the story, Joseph has indeed become our hero. Since his descent to slavery, Joseph has been a model of good behaviour and solid character. The story is now unambiguous in inviting us to regard Joseph, not as an anti-hero, but a hero, as an example for us to follow.

So what is the example he sets for us? Joseph does not withdraw into self-pity, doing nothing, being a victim – a route many of us take when we feel hard done by. 'I am the way I am because so-and-so did this to me, because such and such treats me this way, I am caught in such and such a trap.' We allow ourselves to remain victims, to have our lives dictated by sorry circumstances or by debilitating relationships. We abandon ourselves to living passively because it is easier. That way we don't have to take responsibility for ourselves. The way our lives are is somebody else's fault.

It is easier for any prisoner to become institutionalized than it is for them to retrain and re-equip themselves to take on responsibility in the outside world. Joseph does not choose the easier route. He does not begin acting like a prisoner. Joseph is still his own master. He has retained the power to define who he is. Neither does he indulge in feeling bitter towards God for allowing such an unfair turn of events. He does not give up, concluding, 'God does not reward good character after all.' Instead, throughout his episode in prison, Joseph is remarkably cool-headed and steadfast. What happens is that Joseph chooses to do with this new sphere of influence exactly what he did with his last. Indeed, the very same phrase is repeated from the earlier part of the story: '. . . the Lord was with him and, because of this, Joseph prospered'.

Without a doubt, the storyteller is wanting to hold up the way in which Joseph deals with his second descent and say, 'Here, look at this'. The storyteller is, in effect, putting a rhetorical question to us: 'How is it that Joseph was able not only to survive under such adverse conditions, but even to prosper?' We are being invited to wonder at Joseph's self-sufficiency and his ability to define his character. These are qualities the writer wants us to admire in Joseph and develop in our own lives.

Response-ability

We need to probe further, asking, 'How can I prosper in the midst of adversity and suffering?' 'How can I acquire this great power to define who I am?' One modern-day writer has written about experiences many times more devastating than Joseph's, arguing that each of us has within ourselves the power to do this and refuse to allow circumstances to become our master. The writer's name is Victor Frankl.

Victor Frankl spent the end of the Second World War in a Nazi concentration camp. He had been a University Professor, but the Nazis took everything from him – first his career, then his home, family, friends, wealth. They even took his clothes and his hair. All but one of his family were killed in the gas chambers.

In his utter desolation and humiliation, Frankl speaks of the moment when it dawned on him that the Nazis had not taken from him the one thing that made him a human being. He was still 'response-able'. In other words, he still had the power to choose how he would respond to what was being done to him.

He could abandon himself to despair, hatred and bitterness – the most obvious and the easiest reaction

– or he could choose another way. Frankl realized that he still had the ability to make that choice. So, there and then, he found a way to cope with his circumstances. In his mind he began to imagine what he would say to people when he was freed. Mentally, he began to map out lecture plans on what the Holocaust had taught him about humanity.

Frankl's decision not only helped him to gain courage to survive the trauma of a death camp, but it has given him a testimony that has touched thousands of lives since.

Comparable with such a story of the ability to cope in desperate situations is the story of Nelson Mandela. His imprisonment began in the 1950s, when he was an outlaw – one of a hopelessly outnumbered band of freedom-fighters. Twenty-seven years later he emerged, a national leader with a statesman-like, peaceful air about him. You simply have to admire such steadiness of purpose. Only now do we see the extent to which Mandela must have spent his exile preparing himself for what he believed was to come. It bears comparison with Joseph's transformation – from prisoner to president.

It is sobering to note that we will not acquire the ability to exercise this power to sustain ourselves without experiencing adversity or suffering. Until such a time, the necessary qualities of character remain unexercised, unformed and, in effect, quite theoretical. Suffering is the arena in which these qualities have their opportunity to become real.

The Apostle Paul learned all this for himself towards the end of his career as he progressed from prison to prison. His is not another prisoner-to-president story, but it does present us with a striking example of how a man can choose not to sink into being a victim or self-pity, but even turn his adversity into opportunity.

In his letter to the Philippians, Paul writes, 'What has happened to me has actually served to advance the Gospel!' (Philippians 1.12) Paul is talking of how he used his time in prison to turn himself into an author. The letters he wrote to the young churches as a result of this proved to be of such substance and inspiration that they have been accorded the authority of Scripture. The Church recognized that the calibre of those writings and the extent of their divine inspiration marked them out as being for the whole Church, for all time. This was Paul's heart. Years before he had agreed with the apostles in Jerusalem that the Apostle Peter should work to spread the word to the Jews. He, Paul, would speak to the Gentiles – the rest of the world, in fact. By his authorship of what became Scripture, Paul used imprisonment to serve his life's goal.

Paul's contemporaries also responded positively to his imprisonment. In Philippians we read:

> Because of my chains, most of the brothers in the Lord have been encouraged to speak the word of God the more courageously and fearlessly. (Philippians 1.14)

His followers' fighting spirit was engaged by Paul's response to arrest and imprisonment. His situation brought out the fighter in his partners in the Gospel, and their chosen kind of 'warfare' was to preach the message all the more boldly.

The tension of faith

As this second descent presented a second challenge to the credibility of his early dreams of greatness, Joseph must have re-evaluated them at this point. 'Was I wrong? Were those dreams God's words to me or not?' We can easily judge from his behaviour that Joseph did not opt for despair. Evidently, on this second re-evaluation Joseph still concluded that the dreams were of God, that they were God's word to him, and that even now God was able to deliver. Therefore he concluded that he should not despair, but hold out. After this second forced reappraisal of his faith, Joseph must have held his hope for his future even more resolutely, rooted in a renewed trust in God's word to him, and confidence in God's character. In other words, Joseph was rediscovering his faith.

Each one of us needs to make a similar rediscovery of faith if we are to aspire to Joseph's growing stature as a man. There are times when, as for Joseph, our faith in the promise of God is all we have to sustain us and spur us on.

Thus it is that faith in the promises of God's word in Scripture serves us at times as essential sustenance rather than a comfort, a spur rather than a therapy. There is, in contemporary spirituality, a tendency towards doing exercises and insights that bring comfort to us in an uncomfortable world or offer us escape from the worrying circumstances of life. Some people have their worry beads, some people take drugs, some people chant and some have the comforting tones of the promises of Scripture.

I don't want to rubbish the quietness and strength that meditating on the Scriptures can bring to the heart of any Christian – indeed, there are texts in the Bible written with just such a purpose in mind. However, I want to highlight another approach to the word of God in Scripture. It is an approach that needs reaffirming, an approach to engage the guts of Christian men and engage them in the work of faith. I term it 'standing in the gap'.

Standing in the gap

By 'standing in the gap' I mean learning to use the promises of Scripture differently. The first step is to acknowledge when we find the words of Scripture contradicted by our own experience. What does real faith do when confronted with a gap between the promise of God and our own experience? It does not blindly hope that one day this gap will disappear. It does not abdicate its responsibility to optimism and blithely declare, 'It'll come right in the end'. Faith is not folly. It is not the same as blind optimism. It does not have to ignore the contradictions and gaps our circumstances present it with. What real faith does is best illustrated by the man the Bible calls the 'Father of Faith'.

The Father of Faith is Abraham. The New Testament unpacks the detail of how his faith worked in Romans, chapter four. Paul writes:

> [Abraham] is our Father in the sight of God, in whom he believed – the God who gives life to the dead, and speaks of things that do not yet exist as if they already did. Against all odds Abraham believed, and through that work of faith he became the father of many nations just as he had been told; 'So shall your offspring be!'
>
> Without weakening in his faith, Abraham faced the fact that his body was as good as dead – since he was about 100 years old – and that Sarah's womb was also dead. Yet he was not shaken through doubting God's promise to him, but became stronger in his belief and gave God proper regard, convinced that God was perfectly able to do what he had promised.

Note that the faith Paul describes here is a process. Abraham:

- faces facts
- acknowledges the contradiction
- holds on to God's promise
- chooses to give God his due by trusting God's ability to honour his word.

That process in Abraham's story mirrors the reappraisal that the imprisoned Joseph must have made of his dreams, and details for us how real faith prevails on God to change the realities of current circumstance and bring them into line with the realities his word has spoken of. Real faith, then, is a state of tension for the believer, until he sees the resolution of these conflicting realities.

At times, we will find realities described in Scripture that are presented as normal in the New Testament, but they are perhaps beyond our current experience, unrealized in our own circumstances. Here we find Holy Scripture 'speaking of things that do not exist as if they already did', to use Paul's phrase.

When this happens, rather than ignore the gap, we must choose to stand in it. That is to say, we should make the gap our spur, and the focus of our prayers and actions. This is when we put our faith to work. Facing the fact that things are not as Scripture has presented to us, we must decide to pray and act in such a way that our experience eventually lines up with what Scripture says we should be experiencing.

A good example of a man using this process is that of Oswald J. Smith. In September 1917, while working as a Presbyterian minister in Toronto, Smith began a season of tremendous fruitfulness in his ministry. It began with his daily devotional readings, when he came upon passages that stood in flat contradiction to his personal experience. In August he read Mark 9.23, 'All things are possible to the one who believes.' In

September he read John 15.16, 'I have chosen you and appointed you to go and bear fruit; lasting fruit.'

As far as Oswald Smith was concerned, this was not the way of things. His own experience of ministry suggested another reality. Instead of giving up and letting circumstance become his tutor, Smith, in partnership with a small band in his church, set himself to pray and change the way he worked until he saw a fulfilment of these pieces of Scripture that had so lodged in his imagination.

Alongside the Scriptures, he set before himself heroes from Church history to underline the real possibility of a different reality. In his diary, he notes:

> Lately I have been reading Robert Murray McCheyne, George Fox, Billy Bray, Charles Finney . . . George Whitfield . . . John Wesley . . . John Bunyan, John Smith, David Brainerd and, oh, what men of God they were! What examples of devotion, zeal and piety! Would I could be like them![1]

Smith allowed all these things to spark him into action, coax his spirit back to life – renewing the strength of his faith. He kept those Scripture texts written out in his diary to prod him from day to day. He was learning again to want, and want with a vengeance, the kind of fruitfulness in ministry that the Gospel would lead us to expect. Smith made this his approach to prayer and ministry until, some months later, he saw the beginnings of revival break out in his parish. The impact of his preaching in that time of revival was remarkable. This was the fulfilment of his reactivated desires.

In this kind of way, rather than anaesthetizing our hearts against the discomfort and disappointments of life, the Scriptures and the testimony of our saints and heroes can work to stimulate us and stretch us beyond what we have become accustomed to. This stretch is the work of faith.

If God has ever spoken into your heart or imagination; if there are particular verses of Scripture or dreams or words that people have given you; things with which you resonate and you believe are God's word to you, then you need to hold on to them in the same way God asked Abraham to do in his old age and Joseph in his prison.

EXERCISE 8

If you have become very 'grown up' in your faith, you may need to take some time to think your way through this exercise, to delve back and recall things you felt and believed and were excited by in your spiritual youth. As we have seen, youth is often better at dreaming. If possible, go through the exercise with your pastor or spiritual director.

From the Bible

1 Specifically from your knowledge of the Scriptures, write down two or three key things that you believe God is wanting you to do.

2 Write down any particular ideas in the Bible that hold a special appeal for you.

3 Are there verses you hold on to as personal promises? What were the first verses of Scripture that you can remember knowing or being excited about?

From inspiration

4 Write down anything you feel God has ever spoken directly to you.

5 Write down things other people have said that

---

you believe were 'just right' or inspired. What has God said to you or shown you through others?

From the Church

6 What is your church's vision? What are its ambitions? How do you see yourself fitting into the picture? Has your priest/pastor offered you any guidance in this?

From the heart

7 What do you feel stirred up about?
8 What would you like to do before you die? What one word would you like to be remembered by?
9 What would you like to see change within the next five years?
10 If you can identify unfulfilled dreams and hopes that you believe are from God – such as the verses that captured Oswald Smith's imagination – write them out on some card and set them in your diary or where you pray. Write out a prayer based on them, and resolve to use it in your daily prayer until you see some kind of fulfilment.

Like the exercise in hope, this exercise in faith is a decision for frustration. It involves learning to tap into the fuel of unfulfilled desire and the power of faith. However, I would stress that if this is to be an exercise in faith rather than presumption, it is prudent to bring a measure of discernment and objectivity into the exercise by going through it with your pastor or spiritual director.

Manhood versus youth

Let's just take stock of the virtues the storyteller has already been subtly extolling through Joseph – self-esteem and lack of wrong shame, application as a slave, firm patience during his long years of imprisonment and the ability during that time to sustain his inner strength and define his character. We also observe that Joseph loses his youthful naivety and develops what I call 'social wisdom', in that he has evidently learned to get on with people well.

It is important to understand that these attributes are not merely Joseph's personality traits. They are qualities forming in Joseph as he grows up. They distinguish his adulthood from his youth. In other words, Joseph is getting better as he gets older.

To really take this point on board, we have to reject the implicit message of much popular culture. This is because popular culture in the West extols the benefits of youth to the virtual exclusion of the benefits of growing older. Watch any commercial break on television and you will see very quickly that youth is constantly being paraded for us to covet – the athletic form, the energy, the cheek, the vitality, the wildness, the firmness of body, freshness of complexion and so on. Who, for instance, are the people having fun of orgasmic intensity in the Coca-Cola ads? You don't see middle-aged people exciting each other with Häagen-Dazs in the ice-cream adverts either. No, it is always young people who lead such exciting existences.

This constant message produces in the viewer a creeping anxiety – 'I'm older than those people, and I haven't had that much fun. I can't compete with the vitality of the Coca-Cola people.' 'I don't compare with that youthful body on the screen, that complexion, those teeth. I can't offer that kind of body to my partner now, so what on earth will I have to offer when I no longer have my youth?'

The qualities of youth are held so dear that even older icons are valued for the extent to which they have held on to these attributes. Sean Connery is still an idol because, despite being in his 60s, he has retained something of the form and laddish spirit of a much younger man. He's still a bit of a boy! Tina Turner is still considered sexy because, despite having turned 60, she has the form and vitality of a much younger woman.

This glorification of youth is also repeated in the kinds of films boys tend to watch as they grow up. The icons of heroism in such film-lore are seldom men in full-blown adulthood; men with responsible jobs, a wife, two kids and a mortgage. Surely those are the grey, mundane types our heroes strive to protect. Every young man wants to be a hero somehow. He is excited and enlivened by the thought of heroism. However, the insistent signal, reaffirmed in every boys' film he has ever watched, constantly repeats, 'You won't find heroism in adulthood.' By the time he becomes an adult, the young man will simply believe this is so. This message is a powerfully dispiriting falsehood.

If, like Joseph, we are to get better as we get older, what, then, are the qualities that are special to older age? When I have put it to undergraduate students that being over 30 is infinitely better than being just over 20, they find it virtually impossible to believe. What, they wonder, could they possibly gain by getting older?

A research student once asked me in a psychological test what I liked best about being over 30. To my surprise, I was able to give an extended answer. I said:

Well, I am physically stronger than I have been before. I am in better shape than I have ever been.

70

I smell less. I am more in control of my appearance, I groom myself better. Consequently, I am happier about the way I look. I dress better. I am a better preacher, better counsellor, better listener, better musician than I have been before. I am better at keeping my word. I am better at making conversation. I am better at dealing with situations. I am more in command of myself. I am less easily frightened or manipulated by other people. I am more confident socially. I am more adaptable socially. I have accrued greater tact. I have a better understanding of what sort of person I am. I am better acquainted both with my strengths and weaknesses. I am more discerning. I know better what I want from life. I have already fulfilled a number of ambitions. I am able to think about things more deeply. I know more and understand more than I have ever done in the past.

The student was surprised that there should be so much to say in praise of such an advanced age, but I suspect that many men in their 30s would be able to say something similar. We should give a confident answer to the question 'What are the benefits of reaching adult manhood?' Indeed, we need to answer the question enthusiastically and repeatedly if our young men are to believe they have anything to look forward to in adult life.

The masculine virtues

Thus far, our story has proposed that growth into manhood entails a healthy apportionment of self-esteem, freedom from wrong shame, social wisdom, self-sufficiency, the ability to self-define, steady patience and self-application.

71

These, suggests our story, are some of the masculine virtues. To affirm these virtues as being manly does not imply that they are exclusive to the male and entirely absent in the female of the species. However, I want to suggest that these are attributes that should fire something in the imaginations of men in particular. They are traits to which men in particular should relate.

The women's movement has done much to bring a proper reproach to men as a gender. Old models of the masculine way of being have been rightly rejected. However, this leaves us with the task of rehabilitating the male gender as a worthwhile institution. Men in our society have been left reeling at this tide of criticism, and even feeling a sense of shame at being male. As a gender, we now need to recover confidence that the distinctive attributes of the male are, in fact, positive and important to the proper functioning of a healthy society.

We saw in Chapter 2 how a man's proper self-esteem might be caricatured as foolish pride or conceit. A lack of wrong shame can easily be caricatured as male arrogance. What I have called social wisdom can be parodied as being cynical or manipulative. A man who is strongly self-sufficient can find that he is derided as being full of himself or incapable of being vulnerable. A man who has a strong sense of identity will often find that he is labelled as being stubborn and headstrong. A man who exhibits unshakeable patience can be caricatured as being hard-headed.

The compound caricature of the male of the species is of a being who is proud, arrogant, full of himself, cannot be vulnerable, is headstrong, stubborn and hard-headed. What we need to realize is that these distinctive faults are, in fact, often the flip side of something positive, the shadow of our masculine virtues.

It is important to appreciate that these virtues and

faults are within a hair's breadth of each other. That is why we need to pay special attention to them. We should not confuse faults with virtues – a line needs to be drawn between them. The distinct masculine virtues need to be not erased, but fine-tuned and enhanced, if the male and female of the species are truly to appreciate and value one another as two distinct but complementary genders. Certainly, it is our differentness that we men need to appreciate within ourselves in order to recover confidence as a gender.

Male aggression

Perhaps the most commonly cited male fault is that of aggression. Men are considered brutish and combative. It is so commonly held to be our central flaw, that it is worth looking at this attribute separately.

Debate continues as to the relative importance of nature versus nurture in the formation of gender roles. I am not a professional sociologist or psychologist, so I speak only as an observer, but I find it worth observing that even the most politically correct parents seem to find that, in general, there are certain things that tend to attract the interest and enthusiasm of boys, and certain other things that tend to attract girls. No matter how even-handed we may have sought to become as parents, boys do seem to have more of a bent for speed, cars, trains, spaceships, for contact sports, fighting, guns and other weapons, gadgets, for films involving action, speed, rebels, heroism, war and combat.

Even when we grow up, we continue to enjoy these things. A man's attachment to his car is proverbial. Many movies are crafted carefully for male audiences, containing the various elements that guarantee male 'bums on seats' – elements of content, fast editing, action sequences and heroic central figures. Every decade throws up its own heroic figures – male icons designed to engage the masculine imagination. You only have to think of Tarzan, the Lone Ranger, Flash Gordon, James Bond, Superman, Batman, Indiana Jones, Arnold Schwarzenegger, Jean-Claude Van Damme, Sylvester Stallone.

What do these preferences have in common? What, for instance, does wanting to drive a train have in common with wanting to be like Arnold Schwarzenegger? What does a passion for driving cars have to do with wishing to emulate Indiana Jones? The common thread is that all these ideas key in to a particular element of masculinity that I described in Chapter 3 as man's 'warrior spirit'. It is as if somewhere deep in every man lives a warrior full of energy and looking for a fight. That warrior spirit has to find an outlet if a man is to feel truly alive. It is because that warrior energy is there that men tend to find that they get a buzz from activities and entertainments that entail some kind of combat.

What does this warrior trait have in common with a man's simple pleasures, such as driving, lighting a bonfire, using a power drill? These have to do with a masculine appetite to hold and channel power. It is the urge within him to control or to drive, to strategize or to make things happen, to confront, to combat, to dominate and stake out territory as his own.

This energy is visible in the vigorous clumsiness of boys in their youth. Give them a keyboard and they'll hit it as if it requires force. Set them to a game and it'll become a contact sport with lots of shouting. You can warn them, 'It will end in tears', but that's part of the excitement. Why play any other way? Give them a car and they'll want to drive it too fast, a piano and they'll play it too loud. So, even when handed objects or situations that might require different, more subtle skills, out comes this fighting, power-channelling, masculine drive. This appetite is there in the heart of every man and boy. I generalize, of course, but if this were not the case, then, let me suggest, our cinemas would be screening very different films and our toy shops would be stocked quite differently.

Some would say that if men were not full of such aggressive drives, we might have seen rather fewer wars in our history. That may be true, but I suspect that in the process of trying, in the last generation, to reconstruct the idea of how the male of the species should be, as we have sought to engineer a 'new man', we have 'demonized' male aggression and, as with our other distinctive qualities, thrown the baby out with the bath water.

Certainly it isn't difficult to see how man's warrior spirit can produce unhappy results. For example, when the aggressive drive sets man against man, when the controlling spirit is used by one gender over the other gender or one race over another, when a desire for territory sets gang against gang, nation against nation, class against class or, arguably, political party against political party.

Aggression can be wild and dangerous, but, I want to suggest, this warrior energy emanating from the heart of every man is not wholly bad. We could liken the male aggressive drive to a car. When it is controlled and used intelligently, thoughtfully and well, it is a tremendous boon. It will get you swiftly and safely from A to B. Use it badly or carelessly, however, and it can kill. A car is not necessarily bad, but it is inherently dangerous. The same is true of our aggression. To understand the distinction better, we need to understand the mechanics of the temptation that subverts these energies.

In his letter to the churches, James tells us that 'each

man is tempted when his own appetites are drawn out and enticed.' (James 1.14) The word in the original Greek that I have translated as 'appetites' is *epithumias*. It simply means the natural lusts, desires and drives of a healthy human being. It means our life force. These drives are perpetually seeking satisfaction. The danger is that, unbridled and unchannelled, they are a selfish motivating force. Temptation occurs when, unchecked and undisciplined, these appetites and drives light on doing the wrong thing to meet their need.

In the Gospel, we see Jesus tempted 'in every way as we are' by the exact same process. He had a natural, God-given appetite for food. In the desert, Satan tempted him to use the power of God to satisfy his own personal need to eat. Jesus refused to do this. Similarly, Jesus wanted the worship and obedience of the world. Ultimately, it is indeed the Father's will to put everything under his feet and, being God, Jesus was right to desire these things. Satan tried to subvert this desire by saying, 'You can have it all now, if you will worship me.'

To be tempted, all you need is a desire or an appetite. Even a good desire or appetite can make you vulnerable to temptation.

For instance, a mouse has a God-given appetite for cheese. It is a sign of the mouse's good health that that appetite is there. Nevertheless, that appetite could prove to be the mouse's undoing if it lights on some cheese attached to a sprung mousetrap. In the same way, all our drives and desires may be healthy, but they are also dangerous. They can get us into trouble if we channel them carelessly or if we seek to satisfy them irresponsibly.

There is a right way to satisfy physical appetite, for instance, a right context in which to satisfy your sexual drive, a right arena in which to exercise territorial claims. Likewise, with our aggression. So, although these drives may be enticed, though they may be dangerous, let me suggest that men's drives to control, combat, use strategy, harness, dominate and be territorial are a proper part of adult masculinity. Instead of feeling wrong shame about his aggressive side, a man should, instead, learn to channel his energies correctly and find their legitimate outlet.

For instance, we know that certain male hormones promote aggression. However, we should not as a consequence excuse inappropriate or out of control behaviour by saying, 'Sorry, high testosterone today.' That would be a ridiculous abandonment of responsibility. The proper response to hormones is self-control, and the finding of a healthy outlet for our energies.

Therefore, when aggressive energies express themselves as conflict or war, we should not blame it simply on gender or hormones. We should not resignedly accept guilt as a gender for producing so much testosterone. Instead, we should accept responsibility for bad behaviour on the basis that men are moral beings, capable of choosing good from evil, of channelling our energies correctly. If this were not so, we would not be blameworthy.

When men (and women) channel this warrior spirit into putting a man on the moon, eradicating slavery, fighting injustice, poverty and disease – at whatever level – and preaching the Gospel, then we have tapped well into that aggressive part of our life force. This would seem to be the approach we find in Scripture.

Warrior spirituality

Following on from an Old Testament full of combat, we might perhaps hope to find a New Testament where all is peace and harmony. However, the Scriptures do not propose that a Christian man will find himself in peaceful union with the world around him. In the New Testament, the Christian is unmistakably at war – his warrior energy embraced and engaged 'not against flesh and blood, rather against the principalities and powers of the dark world, against the spiritual forces of evil in the spiritual realm'. (Ephesians 6.12)

The Gospel is certainly not for the person addicted to harmony and oneness with the world. The New Testament calls us to be hostile to the world, despising its temptations. The 'new man' Western society has tried to create is not supposed to be comfortable with such a confrontational stance, but anything else will fail to engage the real passion of men.

Time and again in the Gospels, we hear Jesus calling forth this passion from his followers. He wants their passion to be engaged:

> Whoever acknowledges me before men, I will also acknowledge him before my Father in heaven . . . I did not come to bring peace but a sword. For I have come to turn a man against his father, a daughter against her mother, a daughter-in-law against her mother-in-law – a man's enemies will be the members of his own household. Anyone who loves his father or mother more than me, is not worthy of me; and anyone who does not take his cross and follow me is not worthy of me. Whoever finds his life will lose it, whoever loses his life for my sake will find it. (Matthew 10.32–9)

Jesus wants a man's passion. He wants his warrior spirit. He wants it engaged correctly.

Consider these texts.

> The weapons we fight with are not the weapons of

the world. On the contrary they have divine power to demolish strongholds. (2 Corinthians 10.4)

I do not run like a man running aimlessly, I do not fight like a man beating the air. No, I beat my body and make it my slave. (1 Corinthians 9.26)

I give you this instruction . . . that you may fight the good fight. . . . (1 Timothy 1.18)

To him who overcomes and does my will to the end, I will give authority over the nations . . . [to] rule over them with an iron sceptre. . . . (Revelation 2.26)

Endure hardship with us like a good soldier of Christ Jesus. No one serving as a soldier gets involved in civilian affairs – he wants to please his commanding officer. Similarly if anyone competes as an athlete, he does not receive the victor's crown unless he competes according to the rules. The hardworking farmer should be the first to receive a share of the crops. . . . If we died with him, we will also live with him. If we endure, we will also reign with him. . . . (2 Timothy 2.3–6; 11, 12)

I have given you authority to trample snakes and scorpions, and to vanquish all the power of the enemy. (Luke 10.19)

Can you feel within yourself what parts of the masculine spirit are being evoked by these passages? They are all written to stimulate the warrior within the masculine imagination and engage his fighting spirit. Far from choosing to declare peace, and extinguish that aggressive drive, the Gospel seeks to engage it.

These are elements of Christian spirituality that desperately need to be focused on once more if we are to excite the passionate hearts of men. Spirituality that majors on the passive at the expense of the warrior spirit will leave most men quite cold. It will leave them suspecting that this is not territory for a 'real man' and that such spirituality is really for girls. The 'ballsy' aggressive aspect of Gospel spirituality must be preached, and preached imaginatively and passionately if we are to engage men and masculinity, and see the Church live out the Gospel of Christ in all its radical energy. We underemphasize these elements of New Testament Christianity at our peril if we want our Church to flourish as a community fit for both sexes.

The Christian traditions and our Bible are full of texts, histories and stories set to evoke our fighting spirit. Mariah Woodworth-Etter springs to mind. She was a powerful preacher in the Holiness Movement spanning the late nineteenth and early twentieth century. During her long life, she outlived two husbands and six children. Bereaved of every one of them, she allowed herself no self-pity, but just kept going. Into her 80s she continued as the principal preacher at her Tabernacle Church in Indiana. Neither would she give in as her health began to fail, so indomitable was her spirit. Prior to the Sunday Meeting, two strong men would walk round to the Manse, pick her up in a purpose-built chair, and carry her in it to the pulpit where she would preach as if in her prime. Then she would be carried back after the meeting, the sermon preached.

There's warrior spirit for you. The Church has a wealth of stories like that within the Bible and in its history – stories about men and women that are an absolute gift if we want to coax out the warrior in each of us. Joseph, one such, did not lie down and die when imprisonment came. He did not descend into self-pity.

His warrior spirit was not crushed. The fight he chooses in prison, however, is a more subtle one than he might have chosen in his youth. He doesn't fight against the authority figures set over him or confront the injustice he suffers.

Handling emotion

In prison, Joseph's significant battles would not have been with people, but with his own emotions – against the pressure to slide into becoming depressed or passive. His fighting spirit was engaged in gaol by the struggle to overcome these destructive pressures on his emotional state.

The ability to suppress emotion has, for a long time, been extolled as a stoic virtue in the male of the species. We have taught our boys that 'big boys don't cry'. This saying, long held to be true by our own society, has been called into question in recent times. Men have been told that, actually, they ought to cry, that they should get in touch with their emotions. It can indeed be unhealthy to suppress powerful feelings or to deny how we truly feel. So, we have learned about the proper and healthy release weeping can bring. Certainly, men do need to know how to grieve, empathize and express sorrow. These are elements of real life that we need to go through, and there is a place for weeping in all of them.

Moreover, grief and sorrow must be engaged with if we are to be men of passion in a world crying out for help. This was Jesus' example. The Prophet Isaiah foretold that the Son of God would be 'A man of sorrows and acquainted with grief'. (Isaiah 53.3) Indeed, the Gospels tell us on many occasions of Jesus weeping or 'sighing deeply' or becoming 'deeply troubled' or 'deeply moved'. In the Greek, these words mean something much more full-blown than most translations suggest.

The evangelist Luke tells of one occasion as Jesus approached the city of Jerusalem – a city full of religious people who were refusing to come to him and be saved. He saw this and broke down and wept: 'As he approached Jerusalem and saw the city, he wept over it and said, "If only you knew what would bring you peace – but you cannot see it."' (Luke 19.41–2)

Men could hardly want a more authoritative statement of permission to weep and mourn (an instruction repeated time after time in the Old Testament) than the example of Jesus.

That episode of hurt and compassion immediately precedes the scene of rage when Jesus clears the Temple. Isn't it good to know that when God came to earth, he was not a man of lukewarm spirit, but a man of passion and unafraid to express it?

All this said, we should not be too quick in dismissing wholesale the wisdom of previous generations. The freedom to cry certainly can be a great liberation, but freedom not to cry is also important and also a virtue. Men have long cherished the ability not to be overcome or compromised by feelings. British men have long embraced a horror of being 'soft', 'namby-pamby' or 'wimpy'. The story, too, invites us to admire the stoic, unemotional patience of Joseph as he endures circumstances that might have sunk a lesser man.

Clearly there are times when a man does not want to be subject to his emotions. There are situations when the masculine tendency to cover up natural emotion comes into its own as a tremendous virtue. If a team is about to be led into a difficult situation, the juniors do not want to see their team leader crying with fear, saying, 'I'm not sure I can do this.' To be led positively into battle, a team needs to hear a rather different message. Equally, if the captain of an aircraft suddenly faces instrument failure in the cockpit and is struggling to regain control of the aircraft, he needs to be able to do so clear-headedly, and make a reassuring announcement to the passengers. What the passengers need to hear is the calm, cool voice of the captain telling them, 'Ladies and gentlemen, please fasten your seat-belts, we're going to be experiencing a little turbulence for a while.' They do not want to hear him crying with fear as he makes this announcement. If men are particularly good at suppressing emotion and rising above it, there are times such as these when it is definitely a virtue.

It is this distinctive strength that men are tapping into when they exercise the steady patience necessary to work towards any long-term vision or objective. By definition, a long-term objective is not focused on any immediate return and so the actual route to a long-term goal is not necessarily rewarding in itself. In order to keep on track, being emotional – by which I mean being vulnerable, particularly to negative emotion such as impatience or discouragement – will have to be ruled out. The capacity to set emotions aside and get on is a mark of adult manhood. Youths tend not to have it. Boys are not naturally motivated by the long-term view.

Our society needs this kind of mettle in it if our families, marriages, relationships, businesses, economics and politics are to avoid the further ravages of short-sightedness, impatience and short-termism. Men need to nurture the traits that will give them the patience of a crop farmer, a lighthouse keeper or a sculptor in order to rise above these common pitfalls.

There are times when keeping on track without cracking or giving in will be the necessary channel for a man's distinctive strength. We are not told exactly how many years Joseph was in prison, but we do know that slavery plus prison took up 13 years of Joseph's life – from the age of 17 to 30. He had in all that time to fight against negative emotion and apathy. However, after 13 long years, Joseph's patience paid off, his warrior energy was finally satisfied – with no less a prize than control over the whole of Egypt.

5 BUILDING FOR SUCCESS

Episode 5: The victory

Some time later, the Cupbearer and the Baker of the King of Egypt offended their master. Pharaoh was so angry with them that he had them imprisoned. Now the prison where they were confined just happened to be the Royal Gaol – the very same gaol in which Joseph was held. The two men were assigned to Joseph.

One day when Joseph was doing the rounds, he came upon the Cupbearer and the Baker, who were looking very dejected indeed.

'Why the long faces today?' Joseph asked them.

'We both had bad dreams,' they answered, 'but no one here knows how to interpret them.'

'The interpretation of dreams is God's business,' Joseph replied. 'Tell me your dreams. I know God will give me an interpretation.'

First he listened to the Cupbearer's dream. 'Within three days,' Joseph told him, 'Pharaoh will lift up your head and restore you to your old position. When this happens, remember me and have mercy on me. Mention me to Pharaoh and get me out of this dungeon for I have done nothing to deserve being put in prison.' Then he listened to the Baker. His dream was not so favourable.

'In three days,' Joseph told the man, 'Pharaoh will lift up your head . . . and hang you on a tree and the birds will eat away your flesh.'

Three days later, it was Pharaoh's birthday. To celebrate, he gave a great feast for all his senior staff. He restored the Royal Cupbearer to his position, just as Joseph had foretold, but the Royal Baker was hanged, just as Joseph had foretold.

However, alas, the Royal Cupbearer did not remember Joseph as he had promised. He did not mention him, but completely forgot about him.

Two years later, it happened one night that Pharaoh had two dreams. When he woke up the next morning, his mind was troubled. So he sent for all the fortunetellers, spiritualists and diviners of Egypt. Pharaoh told them all his two dreams, but not one of them could give him a proper interpretation.

Only then did the Royal Cupbearer remember Joseph. When he told Pharaoh about the 'Hebrew prisoner', Pharaoh immediately sent for Joseph to be brought to him. So, they took Joseph out of the dungeon, shaved him, changed his clothes and, when he was presentable, they brought him to Pharaoh. Pharaoh said to Joseph, 'I have had a dream, and none of my people is able to interpret it, but somebody told me that when you hear a dream, you give a correct interpretation. Is that so?'

'I cannot do it myself, O Pharaoh,' replied Joseph. 'It is God who gives me the interpretations. Tell me your dream, and I believe God will give Pharaoh the answer he desires.'

So Pharaoh recounted his dream and Joseph gave the interpretation. 'God has shown Pharaoh what he needs to do. Seven years of great abundance are coming to Egypt. It will be so throughout the land. However, seven years of famine will follow them. They will cancel out the years of abundance and the land will be ravaged. The years of abundance will scarcely be remembered because the famine will be so severe. God gave you the dream in two forms to show that this matter has been firmly decided by God. God will do it soon. Pharaoh must now look for a wise and discerning man and put him in charge over the land of Egypt. Also, you need to set up a Royal Commission to collect a fifth of the harvest over the next seven years and keep the grain in reserve, under Royal Guard. This will be for the Royal Cities come the famine and will enable the country to survive.'

Pharaoh and his staff considered this plan and approved it. Pharaoh then said to his officials, 'Where can we find a man like this, one who has the spirit of God within him?'

Then Pharaoh said to Joseph, 'As it was you to whom God revealed this, I don't think we will find a candidate to equal your wisdom and insight. Therefore, you yourself shall be in charge of my palace. All my people will follow your orders. Only with respect to the throne will I be greater than you. You are now my First Minister.'

Then Pharaoh removed the Royal signet ring and, before all his staff, placed it on Joseph's finger. 'I now appoint you as Royal Chancellor of Egypt,' he said. 'I hereby give you charge of the whole land of Egypt.'

Joseph was dressed in robes of fine linen and wore a gold chain around his neck. He rode in the Royal chariot as First Minister and men would shout before him, 'Make way'.

That is how the great patriarch, Joseph, the son of Israel, came to be the Royal Chancellor of Egypt.

What a fantastic story. By means of a supernatural turn of events, Joseph finds himself more than restored after his 13 years in slavery and prison. For a time, he may have longed to be back in Canaan as the favoured son of his family, wearing his richly ornamented robe, but now he is the favoured son of a whole nation. Now he wears a third robe – a royal robe with a gold chain of office. What a fulfilment of the dreams of his youth.

The key to the happy ending of the story is Joseph's God-given ability to interpret dreams. From the first, we were told that dreams gave Joseph a way of hearing the voice of God. It is this connection with divine wisdom that proves to be Joseph's true greatness. When we first encountered Joseph's inspired dreams, we perhaps recognized in them the potential for the introduction of a dynamic element, not only to Joseph's story but to our own. In this final Episode, we see that Joseph has developed his skills in that area, for now he is able to interpret quite involved dreams for others. Moreover, Joseph seems very assured as he gives his interpretations, first to the Cupbearer, then to the Baker, then to the King. We do not know how much practice he had in advance of this, but he seems pretty confident of his ability to hear what God is saying and of God's ability to speak via the dreams. Once again, the storyteller is presenting us with something we should want for ourselves – spiritual insight.

Spiritual insight

To be a spiritual man – a man of God – surely requires some kind of relationship with God. Episode 5 gives detail to the shape of that relationship for Joseph. As Christians, we have the express promise of God that we, too, will hear his voice, for Jesus said:

> The sheep listen to [the shepherd's] voice . . . he goes on ahead of them and his sheep follow him because they know his voice. My sheep listen to my voice. I know them and they follow me. (John 10.3, 4, 27)

Yet, the whole area of guidance seems to be a perennial struggle for the contemporary Christian. The New Testament writers report, 'The Lord said' and 'The Holy Spirit told us . . .' and we wonder quite how they could have been so clear on the matter. What uncertainty, what hesitation and heart-searchings, what processes of discernment is the writer glossing over? Luke, the writer of Acts, makes hearing from God seem a simple matter. Why, then, is it so much of a muddle for us?

Perhaps our first error stems from wrong expectations as to the nature of God. We could regard the story of Joseph interpreting dreams as if it were there solely to tell us about the unusual abilities of one particular patriarch from Israel's ancient history. However, it may be that the story also tells us something about Joseph's and our God – that he communicates with his people. Indeed, the story's wider context – the Bible – reveals a God who, from age to age, from Old Covenant to New Covenant, persistently speaks to his people. Moreover, in the New Testament, this prophetic connection with God is explicitly for 'all [God's] servants', men and women (Acts 2.18). That is to be the mark of the new covenant. The connection we see between Joseph and God is one the storyteller rightly wants us to desire for ourselves.

Our second error is perhaps in assuming that spiritual insight comes as something blatantly supernatural – such as burning bushes, strangely behaving fleeces, pillars of fire or voices from the sky – like in the Old Testament. However, under the new covenant, the voice of God's will is an altogether more inward thing. 'I will put my law *in their minds*, and write it *on their hearts*' said the prophet (my italics). (Jeremiah 31.33) Sometimes we miss divine guidance because we are waiting for something big and dramatic. We fail to realize that it will be through thoughts in our minds and feelings in our hearts that divine insight is most likely to come to us.

Insight from God is often no more dramatic than a thought from God. It may be a word, a phrase, a dream or a mental picture – just like any other thought or dream. It is not the form that is different, rather the source, the inspiration.

Joseph certainly makes hearing from God appear a simple matter, but how can we possibly aspire to seeing things so clearly? This is not a new question. Indeed, the apostles and the Church fathers have written plenty to steer us through the whole area of hearing from God. In summary, I believe they teach the following three ground rules for listening to God.

Ground rule 1

In day-to-day matters and decisions, take the advice that Paul gives to his young disciple Timothy:

> God has not given us a spirit of indecision, but of power, of love and of a sound mind [*swphronismon*]. (2 Timothy 1.7)

The Greek word *swphronismon*, which we translate as 'a sound mind', literally means 'the capacity to make sound judgements'. Paul is teaching that if you have the Holy Spirit, then you have the capacity to make sound judgements. Therefore, in minor matters, simply do what you believe God is wanting you to do, trusting your *swphronismon*.

Ground rule 2

For matters requiring more inspiration, one great teacher is St Seraphim of Sarov. Seraphim lived in

Russia from 1759 to 1833. He spent most of his life as a hermit in the forests of Sarovka, but when he came out of seclusion, he became renowned as a spiritual director of phenomenal insight. He stood apart from his peers, who wondered at his ability to give inspired words to so many of those he counselled. Seraphim was asked many times about his own ability to speak with spiritual insight, much after the fashion of Joseph. He answered:

> In our days, the words of the Bible seem odd to us, such as . . . those in Acts where it is said that the Holy Spirit, after 'preventing' Paul the Apostle from going into Bythinia, 'sent' him to Macedonia. . . . Some say these texts are incomprehensible, or else deny that man can experience God directly. This incomprehension is due . . . to the lukewarmness of our faith . . . our inattention to God's intervention in our life . . . and the fact that we have lost the simplicity of the early Christians. As for me, as iron committing itself to the smith, I give myself over to God completely. . . . I believe the first word that comes to me to be inspired by the Holy Spirit, and when I start speaking, I honestly don't know what lies in the heart of the person questioning me. I only know that God directs my words for his benefit.[1]

This approach may look like a recipe for disaster, but it agrees with the teaching of many Church fathers, and accords with the teachings of Scripture. It stands in embarrassing contrast to the kind of indecision with which we generally hear God – 'Was that God or was that me? Was that the Holy Spirit or was that just me?' Is that a familiar thought pattern for you, too?

The Apostle James writes directly to people suffering such an internal dialogue:

> The man who doubts is like a wave of the sea, blown and tossed by the wind. Such a man will be forever in two minds, and unstable in all he does. Such a man should not expect to receive anything from the Lord. (James 1.6b–8)

James' answer has the same simplicity of approach as that reported by Seraphim:

> If any man lacks wisdom he should ask God who gives generously to all without finding fault and it will be given him. But when he asks, he must believe and not doubt. (James 1.5, 6a)

Now, James' original listeners were no more infallible that we are in this whole area. That was why he covered the subject. Registering that, we realize that in his churches James would rather see the men behaving boldly, making clear, firm decisions, including the occasional mistake, than have leadership from men who are hesitant, indecisive and perpetually in two minds as to whether or not they really have heard from God. Such a capacity to make firm decisions and stick with them, trusting in our *swphronismon*, even though we may at times be mistaken, might be parodied in men as pig-headedness. However, James is positively extolling the value of such an attitude here.

When Joseph gave his interpretations of the dreams of the Cupbearer and Baker, he cannot have believed himself infallible. Yet, he put forward what he believed God had spoken into his mind, simply and boldly. That is his example to us.

In summary, in matters of medium importance, ground rule 2 instructs us to ask God for wisdom and stick with what we believe, at that point, God has guided us to think.

Ground rule 3

In matters of greater importance, the same approach needs to be taken, but you will need to check out your own conclusions against input from others such as your pastor or spiritual director. St John of the Cross is one who taught the importance of such an approach:

> God . . . does not want you on your own to be relying on communications which you believe to be of divine origin. He does not want anyone to feel assured or confirmed in these matters outside of the context of the Church or her ministers. For God will not bring clarification and confirmation of the truth to an independent believer. Such a person will remain weak in regard to recognizing the truth.[2]

In other words, the only safe place to be seeking the voice of God is within the context of your pastoral relationships within the Church. Individual Christians need to be careful of simply taking their own subjective thoughts and feelings as coming from God or identifying the voice of their own conscience with the voice of God. That is why I suggest that you go through a number of these exercises with your pastor or spiritual director. The expectation of St John of the Cross is not only that we will hear the voice of God in that context, but that we can be assured that his is the voice we have heard.

For modern men to acquire the kind of confidence in the area of divine insight that we see modelled in Joseph requires quite a major shift in mental attitude. That is the purpose of the next exercise.

EXERCISE 9

1 As you read the Bible, note down passages where God shows himself to be a communicating, speaking being.

2 Make a decision of faith, to set your expectations not on the basis of your personal experience to date, but according to the different set of expectations provided by the biblical texts you have written down.

3 Try using the 3 ground rules in your decision making:

- in minor matters, simply do what you believe God is wanting you to – rely on your *swphronismon*
- in matters of medium importance, ask God for wisdom, and stick with what you believe at that point God has set in your heart and mind
- in more major matters, repeat the second approach, but submit your conclusions to your pastor or spiritual director.

By means of this exercise, which, though simple to understand, is the hardest to apply, we are seeking to take as our own, as Seraphim put it, 'the simplicity of the early Christians'. We are seeking a different spirituality, a New Testament spirituality for men.

Tuning in to God

It would perhaps be a mistake to believe that we could duplicate the ministry of a Joseph or a Seraphim simply by copying their methodology. A person's methodology doesn't exist in a vacuum. It flows out of their whole web of beliefs, values and habits. Our story doesn't give us much insight into how Joseph may have fostered his ability to listen to the voice of God. We are left to guess.

However, it's worth noting that both St Seraphim of Sarov and St John of the Cross, who I cited above as authorities in the area of spiritual insight, were men immersed in a daily routine of silence. Both made a priority of long periods of stillness and solitude. I do not believe we can expect such clarity in discerning the voice of God from all the other voices in our head until we have learned to still ourselves and focus our minds in such a way that they are not swimming with a hundred distracting thoughts and images. I believe that if we want to recover a capacity for hearing God, we need to schedule into our lives episodes of silence and solitude. Doubtless, in his long years of imprisonment, Joseph had ample opportunity for both.

You will find in my previous book *Rough Ways in Prayer* (Triangle, 1991) a number of user-friendly exercises that are designed to help you schedule silence and solitude into your own devotional pattern, to help you still your mind. This state of inward stillness is what some of the Church fathers called 'undivided consciousness'. Others called it 'recollection'. Still others 'the state of attention'. Whatever name you prefer, the essence of it is an absence of mental clutter that helps us to become alert to any thought or feeling the Spirit of God might breathe into our waking minds.

The other distinctive aspect of these two great men of God was a passionate commitment to the Holy Scriptures. Their minds and thoughts were totally immersed in the teachings of the Bible. Their imaginations were educated by the values of Scripture.

Seraphim taught, 'A man's mind must swim in the Holy Scriptures'.

His own reading of the Bible was copious. Every Monday he would read through the entire Gospel of Matthew. On Tuesdays, the Gospel of Mark. On Wednesdays, the Gospel of Luke. On Thursdays, the Gospel of John. On Fridays, Saturdays and Sundays, the Acts and the Epistles. This was the man who said, 'I simply say the first thing that comes into my mind, and find it to be inspired'. Of course, Seraphim was a full-time monk and we might struggle to match his volume of reading. However, we cannot expect to have minds schooled for spiritual insight as his was if we will not take the preparation of the mind seriously. This, after all, is the purpose of the Holy Scriptures – to educate and alter our thinking.

When Joseph encountered the dreams of the Cupbearer, the Baker and Pharaoh, his was a mind prepared for the opportunity. Somehow, through his years of slavery and imprisonment, he had fostered and honed the gift he had handled so poorly at the beginning.

Character

What is very interesting is that the trigger to Joseph's ultimate success came from within his own spiritual gift – a gift that he had right from the beginning of the story, even as an unworthy, tactless 17-year-old. This reminds us that our gifts are not dependent on our worthiness. Even in the economy of God, spiritual gifts are never earned – they are always gifts of grace.

Thus it was that Joseph already possessed his genius before he had developed the character to use it wisely. Significantly, the fact of the young man's gift was not sufficient to guarantee his success. In fact, we might almost suspect that God arranged these 13 difficult years for him in order to prepare Joseph for presidency. In that time, he grew up into a man and learned some social wisdom, patience, application, self-determination and spiritual insight. In short, he developed within himself the substance and character that his destined position would require of him. As it was for Joseph, so it is for us. Our gifts are not enough in themselves to guarantee our success. We, too, need to cultivate this thing called character.

It is a matter of general principle in the Kingdom of God that God honours good character. The Bible and Christian tradition is filled with stories that communicate this. The book of Ruth is written almost entirely to teach this point. Similarly, the stories of Daniel, Esther, Tobit. However, let me give you the example of a friend of a friend.

A true story

Back in the 1920s, an Oxford undergraduate felt that God was calling him to become ordained and serve as a priest in the Church of England. He passed the selection process, completed his first degree and was greatly looking forward to the beginning of his training. However, towards the end of his degree, his mother fell seriously ill. The young man made a very painful decision not to enter training, but to look after his mother instead for as long as was necessary. His mother lived for many years as an invalid, nursed by him, and he took a more conventional job to support her. Eventually she died and he completed his career in whatever the field was. However, throughout all those years he had felt deep inside that he was not doing what God had made him for.

At 65, the man retired and emigrated to Canada. He still felt a strong concern for the work of the Church and so, with the blessing of his Vicar, he sought out his Bishop. He explained his story to the Bishop and asked if perhaps he might be trained as a reader or some sort of parish worker. However, the Bishop said, 'No. God has clearly called you to the priesthood. I intend to ordain you.' The Bishop not only ordained the man, but did so without the usual prerequisite of two or three years' theological training, and then put him in charge of a parish.

A friend of mine attended a party thrown for this man just before he died, celebrating his 25 years in ordained ministry – a day he thought he would never see.

That Bishop recognized in the man's story the marks of an honourable and trustworthy character. In entrusting the man with a greater sphere of influence, the Bishop was reflecting God's value system, for the repeated message of the Bible and of history is that God delights in using people like that.

We all want to be used by God, but in our eagerness to be spiritual men, we often rush into religious activism, rather than take the time and effort needed to become the kind of man that God best delights in using. It's worth remembering that even Jesus had to grow 'in wisdom and stature, and in favour with God and men'. He learned under his parents (Luke 2.49–52) and in manual work (Mark 6.2, 3) – 30 years of patient preparation for just 3 years of ministry.

Guaranteed success?

The possession of character means that, whatever your circumstances, you will have the moral and imaginative resources within yourself to keep going and to bring the necessary potential to the situation for something good to happen.

Many think of success as being the power to dominate

your circumstances. However, that is not always possible. We are not always able to control what happens to us. We cannot, for instance, simply decide not to be ill, not to be bereaved or not to be sacked. Although we cannot always be in command of our circumstances, we can determine what potential we bring to them.

Management Consultant Stephen Covey tells the story of a company headed by a very dynamic but dictatorial director. He treated his people as 'gofers', as if they lacked the judgement to make any actual decisions. Consequently, he alienated the bulk of his executive team and they would gather in corridors to grumble about him. However, one of his executives decided not to be defined by his boss's limitations. He, too, was treated like a gofer, but he decided that when he was asked to do something, he would do more than was required. He would anticipate the director's needs, consider the director's underlying concerns and present analysis and recommendations as well as the information that had been requested.

The director was delighted. At the next Board meeting, it was the usual 'go for this' and 'go for that' to all his other executives, but to this man it was, 'What's your opinion?' The man's circle of influence had just grown.[3]

So, we see that the success we cannot guarantee is the roll of the dice in our circumstances. That company executive did not have the power to define the character of the company director. He could not simply give himself a bigger circle of influence. He could, though, determine what he did with the influence already given him.

Similarly, there was plenty of the element of chance in Joseph's circumstances – the cistern where he was thrown 'just happened' to be empty, the Egyptian who bought him 'just happened' to be a royal official, the prison where he was thrown 'just happened' to be the Royal Gaol where the Cupbearer and Baker would be held. Joseph had no control over these events, but he could determine what potential he brought to them. Perhaps the Egyptian who bought him, the prison where he was held and the inmates alongside him could all be seen as turns of good luck. However, as someone once put it, luck can be understood as 'preparation meeting opportunity'. That is certainly true of Joseph's final breakthrough in our story.

Joseph could do nothing to guarantee his own fulfilment or success, but he was able to prepare himself to make the most of every opportunity. Part of Joseph's ascent to manhood was the development of his potential. The lesson is that potential always precedes fulfilment.

Potential precedes fulfilment

Building our potential means taking hold of every opportunity to expand and improve ourselves. That may be in simple ways, like listening to an inspiring person. It may be taking a three-day retreat every quarter. It may be pacing yourself to ensure you have a day off every week. It may be a prioritizing of relationship-building activities, such as recreation with your family or friends. It may be finding a mentor within your church community. It may be creating set-aside time for silence and prayer. It could be to visit a church or organization that could guide or inspire you. These things are often theoretical priorities in our lives. Unfortunately, they have a tendency to remain that way. These kinds of things tend to slip on to the 'I must get round to doing such and such' list. The perennial pressures mean our time becomes dominated by the urgent rather than the important.

To set the building of potential in its proper place requires, first, that we get a proper perspective on our activities. Let me suggest a framework of four types of activity we get involved in.

- **Type 1** activities that are important and urgent, like fixing the faulty brakes on your car or submitting a bid for a contract by a deadline or pulling a child away from a fire. We could call this 'fire activity' – it must be done, and it must be done now.
- **Type 2** activities that are important but not urgent. We could call this 'feeding activity'. It is important that you eat your next meal, but it isn't urgent. You don't have to eat within the next hour or day or few days even, but if you never get around to eating your next meal, you will discover just how important eating is. Eating is seldom urgent, but it is of absolute importance. Similarly, time with our girlfriends, spouses and families, time resting, time learning fall into this category. Anything that feeds us – body, mind or spirit – is in there. These are not urgent activities, nor do they yield an immediate return, but, in the long run, they are essential to our growth and health.
- **Type 3** activities that are urgent but not important – they have to be done immediately if they are going to be done at all, but they are not important. It won't matter that much if they don't get done. 'Paul, you've got 30 seconds 'til *EastEnders* starts.' We could call this 'felt-tip activity'. If I don't put the top on that felt-tip pen in the next minute or so, it will dry up. It is urgent that I act, but if I forget or get called away, then, truly, in the great scheme of things, measured against life and death, war and peace and global

warming, a dry felt-tip isn't of earth-shattering importance.

The telephone always seems urgent. It always rings with the same urgent tone. It seems you have to answer it. However, having answered, it may prove to be unimportant – 'Paul, I just phoned to see what you thought about Bianca's behaviour in tonight's episode of *EastEnders*.'

- **Type 4** activities that are not important and not urgent. They don't have to be done immediately and neither would it matter that much if they were never done. Things like arranging the pencils on my desk in alphabetical order of colour. We could call this 'fiddling activity'.

Urgent and important, fire activities have to happen, and will happen. The gaps that are left between these then tend to be filled in by other urgent activity – by definition, felt-tip activity. In the time remaining, we often coast along in displacement or fiddling activity. That is how Type 2, feeding activity, is squeezed out. As it has no immediate return, it gets deprioritized and finds a resting place on the back-burner. Yet it is feeding activity that, in the long run, enables us to prosper, to sustain our drive and build potential in the way that Joseph managed even within the confines of prison.

Practically speaking, there is only one way to ensure that this happens – to identify your own feeding activities and timetable them in advance into your diary. Think of them as appointments that you must keep as seriously as any other appointment. To do this, you must convince yourself of their true importance. Talk to anyone who has experienced some crisis in their health or a family break-up and you may decide more resolutely not to learn the hard way the importance of giving your health or your family their proper priority.

Programme feeding activity into your diary and keep those appointments, without fail.

Carl Jung tells the story of a man who was seeing him for counselling. The man wanted to see Jung at a particular time on a particular day. 'I'm sorry,' said Jung, 'but I have an appointment at that time.'

When the two met together the next time, the client was furious. 'You told me that you had an appointment on Tuesday. But I happened to see you. I know exactly where you were and exactly what you were doing. You were sitting on the bank on the river, doing nothing other than dangling your toes in the water!'

'That's right,' said Jung. 'It was my appointment with myself. And I NEVER break it!'

Jung understood the importance of scheduling feeding activity into his diary with all seriousness.

EXERCISE 10

1 Make a list of Type 2 activities. These are activities that you are convinced are long-term important things for you. Consider what will happen to you and your development if these activities do not occur.

2 Find one occasional activity (a retreat, fishing trip, conference, visit to an organization or mentor) and schedule it into your calendar right now.

3 If you don't already use a diary to organize your time, start using one. At the beginning of each week, timetable in one or two feeding activities that will:

- help to sustain you – emotionally, physically, spiritually
- help to continue to build your potential.

4 Tell a friend what these two goals are and why.

The added pressure of accountability to your friend will be a boon. Better to be bullied by a friend into doing what you have set yourself than, unembarrassed, continue sawing with something that's actually getting blunter.

Through the course of the story, Joseph has been lifted up three times – once by his master when he was a slave, once by his Prison Warder and once by the Pharaoh. All three breakthroughs happened because the people around Joseph recognized the quality and character of the young man. Indeed, his potential was recognized and rewarded even in the most unpromising of circumstances. Instead of these circumstances defining Joseph, we see that they were turned around because of the unmistakable potential he had within him.

In slavery, Potiphar recognized his calibre. Joseph proved himself to be trustworthy, and so he was given maximum fulfilment within the scope of Potiphar's estate. In prison, the Warder recognized Joseph's character. Joseph showed himself to have grown in patience and social wisdom and was rewarded with privileges within the limits of the Royal Gaol. The third and final breakthrough came when Joseph showed himself to be a man of genuine spiritual insight – so much so that even Pharaoh, a man of a different religion and a great leader himself, recognizes Joseph for what he is – a man of God. Thus, Joseph finds himself accorded the highest office of one of the world's great powers.

The first two breakthroughs taught Joseph that God honours good character, that potential precedes fulfilment. However, they were to prove to be merely a preparation for Joseph, a taste of his final royal ascent, his great success – the victory for which history would remember him.

CONCLUSION:
SPIRITUALITY FOR MEN

In the last five chapters we have seen how the story of one man's journey can be used to stimulate something in the imagination of the believer and propose new values and aspirations.

The story of Joseph is just one of the Bible's many character portraits of men in leadership. Indeed, a substantial proportion of the Old and New Testament is written with men in mind. It isn't that the Bible is concerned with spirituality for men only, but rather that it was chiefly through the obedience, initiative and spirituality of men that the authors of the Scriptures expected their teaching to shape society at large.

The Bible is culturally quite foreign to the West of today in its bias to the masculine. However, it is the very foreignness of the Bible, coupled with the inspiration of the Scriptures, that enables the Bible to speak from beyond the shifting boundaries of our own culture and to speak with authority. That is what gives an edge to the teaching and mythology of the Bible in the shaping of gender identity and spirituality.

The masculine bias of the Scriptures means that, when it comes to exemplars, it is unsurprising that we find the Scriptures filled predominantly with stories of male heroes and anti-heroes. It isn't that men can't learn important and inspirational things from women. Indeed, earlier we cited Mariah Woodworth-Etter as an outstanding model of warrior spirit for men to emulate. Rather, it is that there is a unique place in the masculine imagination for male role models.

Ancient societies recognized the need to present their young men and boys with positive images of adult manhood. For this purpose, from East to West, stories and fables have grown up that have strong, heroic images of adult masculinity to inform and excite the imaginations of young men and boys, to shape their understanding as to what the nobility of a man can and should consist of. Contemporary Western society's lack of such a coherent mythology leaves today's young men with a gap in their psyche where such positive images and understanding should be.

Almost every ancient culture has its stories and myths – like the story of Joseph – that are there to teach its young men how to become fulfilled, adult men. From East to West, these mythologies are largely of three kinds – tales about kings and princes, hunters or warriors and farmers. The broad thrust of these stories is that, to make yourself a real man, you will need to build within your own character the self-esteem and sense of identity of a prince or king, the imagination and fighting spirit of the warrior and the strength, self-sufficiency and steady patience of the farmer. Joseph's is such a story and, interestingly, it holds together something of all those elements.

However, the story of Joseph is not a complete tool-kit for male initiation. It is only one of countless stories within the Scriptures and writings of the Christian tradition. All through the ages, the Church has treasured the stories of its heroes to teach its people – men and women – just what it is they should be aspiring to. However, it is not just the Church that knows about the spiritual and imaginative need within people for heroes and role models.

Writing in the early 1980s, Thomas Peters and Robert Waterman, Junior, observed the same pattern of behaviour in the world of big business. In their seminal book *In Search of Excellence* (Harper & Row, 1982), they analysed how successful businesses go about motivating a creative spirit within their workforces. Large corporations have an innate tendency for institutionalism and regulation that demotivates the wild, creative spirit of the individual worker. Thus, the initiative and energy that might have spawned the success of a company in its early days can be squeezed out of the present workforce.

The excellent companies seek to reinforce the value of individual initiative and experiment by carefully nurturing a company mythology. Stories are created and repeated about figures from the company's history, who, by individual initiative, experiment and boldness, advanced the company in some startling way.

The intention is that the myths and stories help to evoke the same kind of creative and pioneering spirit within the current generation of workers so that they might each respond by thinking, 'I could be like that, too.' This is essentially the purpose of the veneration of saints.

The veneration of saints

The veneration of saints, or the 'cult of the saints', is an element of the Christian tradition that has often been derided as naive and unhelpful. Certainly when saints are presented as specimens of inhuman perfection there is, without doubt, a demotivating aspect to it. When we tell of our saints as if they were a race of inaccessibly good people, glittering with goodness utterly beyond the reach of our own efforts, those listening might legitimately shrug their shoulders and conclude, 'Obviously they were a different type of person. Clearly they were made of different stuff to me.' The result is that the normal Christian will not expect God to use him in anything like the way he used these other saints.

Thus, in cultures that set their saints up on a kind of pedestal, the normal Christian, instead of expecting God to use him to perform great feats, ends up expecting it to be the saints in heaven – whom God used greatly while they were on earth – to be the ones who will continue to perform such feats on behalf of the Church on earth. I call this 'hyperveneration'.

Certainly it is good to venerate our heroes, but it is bad if we who are alive abdicate our responsibility for greatness to those who have done their bit already and gone before us. After all, Scripture does not say, 'These signs shall accompany those who are dead', but, rather, 'those who believe' (Mark 16.17).

Similarly, Hebrews does not read 'Therefore, since we are surrounded by such a great cloud of witnesses, let them do the hard work'. Rather, it says, 'Therefore, since we are surrounded by such a great cloud of witnesses, *let us run the race marked out for us*' (italics my own; Hebrews 12.1). In other words, the great feats the New Testament sets before us and the saints continued, are now the responsibility of the normal living Christian.

Disveneration

At the Protestant end of the Church, at times the opposite kind of imbalance has developed, which I call 'disveneration'. We prefer to emphasize the faults and fallibility of our great saints (we might not even use the word 'saint'). We want to stress that it is normal people just like us, riven with faults and failings, whom God wishes to use.

That is true. If it were not so, the work of the Kingdom would be in big trouble. However, casting our saints as anti-heroes simply does not do justice to the kind of people God has most powerfully used through the ages. As we saw in Chapter 5, God 'delights' in using people of good character.

If we simply ignore the fact that those men whom God has used most notably have all been single-minded, purpose-led individuals, then we may very well miss the key to our own greatness. If we casually gloss over the self-sustaining spirit of these people, the firmness with which they chose to stand apart from the prevailing culture of their society, then, again, perhaps we are missing the real key to our own success or failure.

It is as lazy and as naive as the error of hyperveneration to cast the saints as people just like us because, invariably, in one way or another, they were not. They were not perfect, but they had particular qualities and attributes that we too will need if we are to bear fruit in anything like the way they did. Also, today, we need to appreciate that their stories have been recorded to shake us out of the complacency with which we often accept our own muddling efforts to extend God's Kingdom.

Their stories have been handed down from one generation of teachers to the next in order that we might be inspired to stretch ourselves beyond that which we already are. If we tell their stories well, then we shall be reactivating our imaginations with an inspiration that is entirely necessary to shake us out of the unfulfilled, unmanly apathy into which modern Christian men have sunk in comparison to the most notable of our forefathers.

In the Church, we have an advantage over society at

large as we seek to reactivate the imagination of our young men. It is that we have a wealth of heroes and exemplars to set before one another. Their stories are there to show us what spirituality can and should look like in a man. In Chapter 3, we did an exercise in which we allowed our own hero figures to put us back in touch with our own aspirations to greatness, and that is the true purpose of the veneration of saints.

The story of Joseph has put forward a number of virtues and qualities for men to aspire to – peacock spirit, freedom from wrong shame, social wisdom and spiritual insight, ability to self-define, steady patience and properly channelled warrior spirit. These are not qualities unique to the masculine, but I believe that there is a unique way in which men relate to those qualities.

For the veneration of saints and Bible heroes to work, their stories have to be told – and told imaginatively. It is the telling of the story that stimulates the imagination – the story excites the imagination to aspire. The aspiration, when it becomes heartfelt, provides the motivation necessary for the building of character and potential for fulfilment. That is the true purpose of the cult of the saints. That is what happens when we preach our faith well – it stretches us beyond that which we already are.

There are countless figures from Christian history who motivate me in that way, but, as I mentioned earlier, there are four in particular who have been special to me: Paul, St John of the Cross, St Seraphim of Sarov and Charles Simeon. These four people set a positive vision of adult manhood before me. To me they are inspiring men of God. I have pictures of them on my study wall as a perpetual stimulus for me to stretch myself beyond that which I already am. Now neither Joseph nor the other four men I have named were perfect.

The storyteller did not write Joseph's weakness out of the story. Neither has the passage of time removed all trace of the humanity of the other four. However, all five figures, while flawed, excelled in one area or another and in a way that gives me something to aspire to. Indeed, the vision that these figures have conveyed would be sufficient to keep me going for a lifetime. We also have the choice of countless other exemplars and role models to stimulate, inspire and reactivate our inner drives towards fulfilment. The stories are there to be put to work.

In the Church we have another advantage. Christians tend to read books. They also attend conferences, retreats, house parties, conventions, cell groups and seminars, and, week by week, they listen to the preaching of the Bible. This means that we already have in place many structures by which vision and passion can be disseminated to shape an inspired, aspiring and active community.

Alongside the one-to-many media of pulpit, platform and print – along with radio and TV – there is great potential in the Church for networks of relationships to develop by means of which older men can give to younger men the vision and confidence they need. I say 'potential' because, often, our churches are not the networks of relationships they ought to be. A great weakness of the Church in the West today is the extent to which we treat church as if we were individual customers consuming a product. However, it can be something much more altruistic and life-giving than that.

The main business of any church must not be keeping customers satisfied – it has to be that of making disciples. That, after all, is the Great Commission left to the Church by Jesus himself. This means that, as Christian men, we have to take personal responsibility to know God and know the faith well enough to disciple our young people; to lead our young men forward in their relationship with God to a place of greater fulfilment as Christian adults. This can only work at the level of real one-to-one relationships.

Transforming leadership

The business world was learning to apply this principle of one-to-one or intimate discipleship back in the 1980s. It was commonly called 'transforming leadership'. Leadership Consultant J. McGregor Burns described it this way:

> Transforming Leadership occurs when . . . leaders and followers raise one another to higher levels of motivation and morality. Their purposes become fused. . . . Leaders throw themselves into a relationship with followers who will feel elevated by it and . . . become more active themselves, thereby creating new cadres of leaders.[1]

That was the pattern of leadership by which Jesus turned the world upside down. Jesus was a transforming leader who took 12 ordinary men and changed them into powerful men of God. By means of his input, the 12 themselves became leaders of men in turn. They became powerful and persuasive men, passionate to the point of giving their lives in the endeavour of making disciples. It was by throwing himself into an elevating relationship with them that Jesus stretched them beyond what they already were. I believe that the young men in our Church today are hungry for such transforming leadership.

Let me return to the words of veteran youth worker, Wayne Rice:

Our young people need to be surrounded by adults. The reason young people are getting into so much trouble today is [that] there are no adults out there. There is no one they can lean on or look up to, or model themselves on. . . . In cultures of the past, youth had rites of passage which moved them from childhood to adulthood. Following these rites of passage, the youth would be embraced by the adult community and there would be a place for them in the adult world. This is no longer true for our [young people]. . . . The challenge for the Church is how to make that happen for our kids. . . . The Church's job is to surround our . . . young people with Christian adults they can look up to and model themselves on. They don't have to be perfect or anything, they just need to be there.[2]

At the moment, there is a vital need and a hunger among our young men to get input of this kind from older men. This was what our hero Joseph desperately needed as he turned 17. He needed a proper welcome to the adult world. Perhaps such an initiation could have saved him 13 years of frustration.

The current lack of male initiation and welcome within our own society not only leaves individual men with a personal deficit, it leaves our society lacking the distinct input that should be coming from the male of the species. It leaves the Church with a lack of healthy aggression and warrior spirit in its leadership. It makes for a limp, apologetic, shuffling kind of Church, quite unattractive to any self-respecting man. Learning to welcome our young men into adulthood is not just a matter of enriching individuals, but of building the future character of our Church and society.

The 'Philemon six principle'

If we really want to 'put some balls back' into our Church and society, the power to do so is easily within our grasp. We have the means to be making men of God.

All it needs is for the kind of men who read this book to take the initiative to form positive, nurturing relationships with the generation coming up. It simply requires us to reject the now conventional segregation of generations and age groups and attend to giving our young men an enthusiastic, informed and encouraging welcome into the adult male world – into our world.

Working with students over the last ten years has shown me the value of giving such attention to people. Dedicating time to building a relationship with a young person, to bless them and build them up, does wonders for their level of self-confidence. Without self-confidence a young person will lack the inner resources to apply anything I might wish to teach him. With self-confidence, however, comes the impetus to expand and flourish.

If we men who are a little older will labour to give our young men a bit of self-esteem and peacock spirit; if we will teach them proper shame and seek to liberate them from wrong shame . . .

if we men will teach them to sustain and define themselves and attend to building their potential . . .

if we will affirm them as they begin to enter into the contradictions of life and the tension of faith . . .

if we will teach them how to channel and use their inherent aggression and warrior spirit . . .

if we will help them to grow in social wisdom and spiritual insight, teach them not to reject but to reappraise their dreams and desires . . .

if we will confidently extol the virtues of adult masculinity and reassure our young men with enthusiasm that there is something great to look forward to as they leave their youth and commence the journey of adult manhood . . .

. . . then we will have met the needs of today – we will be teaching a spirituality for men.

The key change has to happen at the level of our man-to-man relationships. Young men need to see these qualities with their own eyes if they are to take them on. In the final analysis, if it is the fear of a 20-year-old that at 35 the male of the species is an inexorably dull, half-dead kind of creature, the best and only real assurance possible is for him to know a 35-year-old who is not inexorably dull and half-dead, and to receive teaching and encouragement from him.

Now you might say to me, 'But, Paul, that's what I need.' So, let me, in conclusion, point you to a golden principle from the Bible, one I call the 'Philemon six principle'. It comes from a short letter written by Paul and Timothy to a man called Philemon. It has only 22 verses in it, and this is what the sixth one has to say:

> I pray that you will be active in sharing your faith, so that you may come to a full grasp of every good thing we have in Christ.

I believe the proper application of that verse is to evangelism. That is, as we each share our faith with others, our knowledge and understanding of the benefits of that faith will grow, deepen and become more real.

However, I believe that there is an underlying principle here that we can apply more widely. The words that follow are not a translation of the Philemon text, but a parallel statement. What follows is not Paul's prayer for Philemon, but mine for you, as you seek to make a difference.

I pray that you will be active
in sharing your confidence and belief,
in order that you yourself may come to a full grasp
of every good thing that is ours as men of God.

I for one am confident that the Philemon six principle is true. I certainly find it to be so. In case you haven't yet guessed, it is the very reason for my having written this book.

References

Chapter 1

1 Wayne Rice, from an article in *Youthwork* magazine, October/November 1994, Elmhouse Communications, New Malden, Surrey.
2 Robert Bly, *Iron John*, 1990, Element Books, Shaftesbury, Dorset.

Chapter 2

1 Ruby Wax, video *Wax Acts*, Central Independent Television PLC, 1992.

Chapter 4

1 Oswald J. Smith, *The Passion for Souls*, 1983, Lakeland Books, Basingstoke.

Chapter 5

1 St Seraphim of Sarov – sources:
St Seraphim of Sarov, 1975, Valentine Zander SVS Press, Crestwood, New York.
Little Russian Philokalia, 1978, St Herman of Alaska Brotherhood, Platina, California.

2 St John of the Cross, *Selected Writings*, 1987, SPCK, London.
3 Story taken from Stephen Covey, *The Seven Habits of Highly Effective People*, 1992, Simon & Schuster, London.

Conclusion

1 Thomas J. Peters and Robert H. Waterman, Jr., *In Search of Excellence*, 1982, Harper & Row, London.
2 Wayne Rice, from an article in *Youthwork* magazine, October/November 1994, Elmhouse Communications, New Malden, Surrey.